To Jenny
Best wishes, happy decorating

Tomsi Peda.
10. 9. 94.

Happy Fuy Making !!!.
lots of love

Alan Dunn

BEST WISHES
Tony Warren

Decorative Touches

TOMBI PECK

MEREHURST

DEDICATION

This book is dedicated to the men in my life!
To Christopher and Alasdair, my two
grandsons; and to Tony Warren and Alan Dunn
for all their help in the production of this book.
Thanks guys!

ACKNOWLEDGEMENTS

I would like to thank the team who have helped put the book together. In particular I would like to thank Barbara Croxford and Sue Atkinson for their kindness, patience and good food!

My undying thanks must go to Tony Warren who coated most of the cakes and boards in the book and whose beautiful royal icing work enabled me to include this section in the book – I have the knowledge, but not the skill! To Alan Dunn who spent weeks with me keeping me going with his unstinting help – who else would have made $3\frac{1}{2}$ THOUSAND ivy leaves for a friend – dusted, glazed and veins scraped! He also helped make many other leaves and flowers, not all of which can be noted here.

I am most grateful to my friends Jenny Walker and Norma Laver from A Piece of Cake for supplying me with all the flowerpaste for the book. It is, in my opinion, the best on the market.

My thanks to Mr. Nutkin from Sugar Flair for allowing me to buy the petal dust in large quantities – also to Squires Kitchen for the large tubs of paste colours and dust; to Judy and David Hunniset from Cake Creations for supplying South African Hi-liters; to David and Margaret Ford of Celcakes for the beautiful perspex stand specially made for my daughter Maggie's wedding, and for supplying the celpots and celpicks used in the book; to Sally Harris of Tinker Tech 2 for making and providing the metal cutters; to Joan Mooney of Great Impressions for making and in some cases supplying the veiners; to Della Marcel for the basic idea of the filet crochet extension work and to Pauline King and Anne Brownlow for introducing me to elephants!

Published in 1994 by Merehurst Limited, Ferry House,
51–57 Lacy Road, Putney, London SW15 1PR

Copyright © Merehurst Limited 1994

ISBN 1 85391 367 7

A catalogue record of this book is available from the British Library.

Designed by Maggie Aldred
Photography by Sue Atkinson

Typeset by J&L Composition Ltd, Filey, North Yorkshire

Colour Separation by Global Colour, Malaysia
Printed and Bound in Italy by G Coualt & C SpA

CONTENTS

Introduction – A Brief History of
Cake Decoration   4

SUGAR FLOWERS   7
Country Wedding Cake: 8
Periwinkle, Briar rose, Honeysuckle,
Bittersweet, Black bryony, Variegated
and dark ivy, Birdsfoot ivy
White Beauty Wedding Cake: 18
Stephanotis, Rose, Dendrobium
orchid, Ruscus, Longiflorum lily
Pink Rose and Gardenia
   Wedding Cake: 30
Wired gardenia, Chinese jasmine,
Wiring of waterfall sprays, Coffee flower
Porcelaine Wedding Cake: 40
Freesia, All-in-one rose, Quick
lily-of-the-valley, Java orchid
African Wedding Cake: 48
Agapanthus, Rosy cheeked lovebirds,
Eucalyptus leaves, Silver tree,
Devil's root, Erica, Impala lily,
Shepherd's delight, Bridal gladiolus
Christmas Rose Cake: 58
Christmas rose
Patio Perfection Cake: 62
Nasturtium

DRIED AND PRESSED
FLOWERS   66
Dried Flower Arrangement: 68
Chinese lanterns, Lotus seedheads,
Pearl grass, Poppy seedheads
Harvest Cake: 72
Twigs, Larch cones, Acorns,
Rose hips, Honesty, Oak and Beech
leaves

Pressed Flowers: 80
Pansy or viola, Potentilla, Fuchsia,
Primrose, Forget-me-not
Pressed Flower Card   84
Trinket Bowl   85

BONSAI   88
Flowering Cherry Bonsai   91
Wisteria Bonsai   94
Hazelnut Bonsai   97

PASTILLAGE   100
Oval Box   102
Passion Flower Cake: 103
Passion flower
Victorian Decoupage: 106
Victorian Decoupage
   Christening Cake   108
Hearts and Flowers
   Engagement Cake   109
Enamelled Easter Egg   112

SUGARPASTE   114
A Mother's Day Gift: 116
Cyclamen
Waterlily Pram Cake   121

ROYAL ICING   125
Damask Rose Cake: 126
Damask rose
Brush Embroidered
   Magnolia Cake: 130
Magnolia
Curious Cats   135

Techniques   138
Templates   141
Index   144

A BRIEF HISTORY
OF
Cake
Decoration

It is very difficult to put an exact date on when baking, cake making and decorating began, although it is thought that the Babylonians taught the Egyptians the art of baking. A painted panel of around 1175 BC, depicting the court bakery of Rameses III, illustrates the preparation of several types of cakes as well as some bread. There are also indications that confectionery sweetened with sugar was on sale in Egypt around 700 BC.

The tradition of creating special cakes for weddings goes back to Roman times. The cake was crumbled over the bride's head so she would be blessed with abundance. This tradition was brought to Britain by Julius Caesar in 54 BC and persisted in various forms until 200 years ago. Now each guest is given cake.

An essential ingredient in the development of cake making and decoration, cane sugar, is thought to have originated in India. From here it moved westward to Mesopotamia, where it grew well in the area between the Tigris and the Euphrates (the biblical setting of the Garden of Eden). As this was an area where almond trees flourished, it seemed inevitable that a food made from both ingredients – marzipan – should emerge from here.

Decorated cakes made their first appearance in England during the reign of Elizabeth I. Most were adorned with moulded almond paste pieces. Sweetmeats were served in dishes moulded from a form of pastillage.

In 1609 the first recipe for sugarpaste was published in a book by Sir Hugh Platt, entitled *Delights for Ladies*. This paste was made from 'fine white sugar, starch and gum tragacanth', coloured and flavoured with pounded flowers.

Sugar sculpting began in Italy in the seventeenth century. Giovanni Lorenzo Bernini used sugar to create works of art for special occasions. Not until the 1760s were the constituents of our present-day celebration cakes put together. The first edition of Mrs Raffald's book *The Experienced English House-keeper* (1769) contains three successive recipes for a rich cake, marzipan and icing. Another recipe for icing for a wedding cake was given by the cookery writer Elizabeth Moxton in 1789.

The most celebrated confectioner of this time was Antoine Careme. His book *Patissier Royal* is illustrated with engravings showing that he used a form of pastillage for these structures. A similar recipe for pastillage was given in the book *The Complete Confectioner* by Frederick Nutt in 1819.

In 1894 Ernest Schulbe first competed at the London Exhibition. He remarks in his book, *Advanced Piping and Modelling*, that at this time very little 'net or string work', as he described it, was done in Britain. Schulbe's book shows us that the modelling tools we know today were in use in the last century, though made of bone rather than of plastic. Flowers were modelled in a similar fashion, including the use of stamens. The paste used was a mixture of marzipan and gum paste. Brass crimpers, very similar to those on sale today, were also used.

Very little was published on cake decorating between the two World Wars. The Second World War, with its severe sugar rationing, reduced the number of books being published on the subject still further and icing practice became very difficult. Mashed potato was used to keep piping skills honed. One pound of icing would be used for a whole cake decorating class, for weeks at a time. Although there were sugar restrictions in the colonies during the War, they were not quite as stringent as

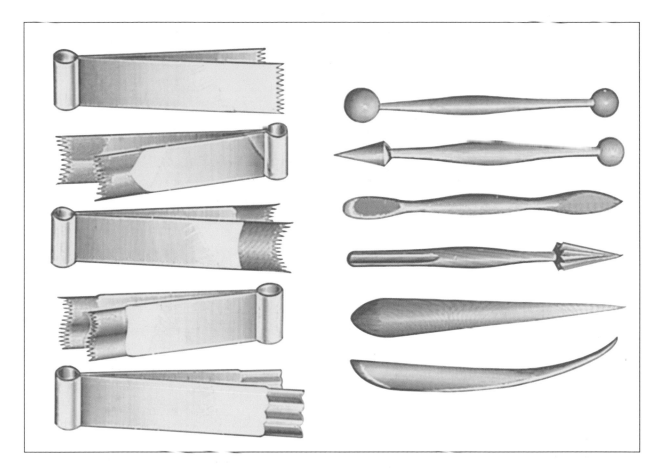

Marzipan pincers and wooden modelling tools. From
Advanced Piping and Modelling *by Ernest Schülbe, 1906.*

in the United Kingdom. Sugarpaste was the preferred covering of rich fruit cakes in countries like Australia and South Africa.

In Britain, the master bakers continued with their favourite technique – royal icing. Ronnie Rock, one of the greatest craftsmen, actually ground his own icing sugar to produce the magnificent piece he made for the first post-war exhibition in 1946. It is now at the National Bakery School, London.

Many other talented artists and craftsmen have enriched the field of cake decorating since then. A father and son, Edwin and F.E. (Freddie) Schur should be mentioned. Edwin Schur was renowned for his magnificent sugarpaste sculpturing. He developed many interesting techniques and produced a wide range of finely carved wooden moulds. Freddie Schur, when he worked for Huntley and Palmer, was responsible for one of Queen Elizabeth II's wedding cakes. He also made an ornament for one of Princess Margaret's.

The 1970s and 1980s were enriched with the work of Colin Burge, which was on show at the Salons Culinaire up and down the country. His figure modelling is the best we have seen. Evelyn Wallace, the author of *Cake Decorating and Sugarcraft*, taught in Adult Education Centres. She was responsible for popularizing this marvellous craft, and it was she who coined the word 'sugarcraft'.

During the 1980s I joined forces with Elaine and Stuart MacGregor to persuade manufacturers to produce the products we needed. Jimmie Winterflood was instrumental in getting Renshaws to produce Regalice (named by Stuart). Mr Nutkin at John Bond Inks listened to our requests for food colours and in due course produced the Spectral range. Gerry Harris formed Tinker Tech and began making the first metal flower cutters.

With the formation of the British Sugarcraft Guild and new products becoming available, the revitalization of cake decoration began.

SUGAR FLOWERS

Sugar flowers are what first attracted me to cake decorating. My grandmother, Chloris Browne, moulded some beautiful arum lilies for a cake at a wedding where I was the bridesmaid. I was just 8. I was hooked!
I started making sugar flowers myself when I had young children. When I reached Great Britain I was astounded that I could find no-one using this form of cake decoration. I started teaching sugarpaste and flower making in Thame in 1978. In 1979 I was introduced, by Denise Fryer, to the use of wires in flowers and dusting to achieve beautiful soft effects.

Country
WEDDING CAKE

*20 cm (8 inch) and 28 cm
(11 inch) oval cakes
28 cm (11 inch) and 36
cm (14 inch) oval cake
boards
Pale green sugarpaste
Ivory royal icing
Petal dusts
Offset perspex cake stand
46 cm (18 inch) length of
new broomhandle set into
a 15 cm (6 inch) base
Ivory picot-edged ribbon
for board edge*

•

FOR THE SPRAYS
*30 sprays of birdsfoot
ivy, some long,
some short
3 sprays of bryony
18 sprays of briar rose
6 sprays of bittersweet
9 sprays of fly
honeysuckle
2 sprays of honeysuckle
6 sprays of periwinkle*

Make sure the rod is
securely stuck into
the base or the
whole arrangement
could come apart
during transit.

This is a wedding cake for those who love creating flowers. There is, however, a brush embroidery pattern which can be incorporated with the cake if preferred.

♣ Cover the cakes and boards with green sugarpaste. Cut templates from the cake tins used. Place the templates on the boards where the cakes will be positioned, then remove the sugarpaste from this section. Crimp the edges of the boards with an appropriate crimper. Leave to dry. Place the cakes in position on the boards. Pipe a fine snailtrail around the base of the cakes. Attach the ribbon to the board edge.

♣ If you would like to decorate the cake with brush embroidery, first transfer the tracing (see page 141) to the top or side of the cake and follow the instructions as described in Magnolia cake on page 130. (This should, of course, be done when the cake has been freshly covered and is dry.) Start with the pieces that appear furthest away, working forwards gradually to the flowers that form the foreground. Carry out the brush embroidery in ivory, highlighting the colours delicately with a little petal dust.

♣ The central spray is made up using long trails of all the flowers and foliage. I use birdsfoot ivy, bryony, briar roses, bittersweet, fly honeysuckle, ordinary honeysuckle and periwinkle. Start with sprays of ivy, then add the bryony, bittersweet, briar roses, ordinary honeysuckle and

lastly fly honeysuckle and periwinkle at the base of the stand. Keep fastening the trails in place with pieces of very fine silver florist's wire. Tie it loosely around a section, making sure it will not crush any flowers or leaves, and then at the back of the pole twist a folded piece of wire until it pulls in tight against the pole.

♣ The two smaller sprays are wired up to look as informal as possible, using a complete selection of flowers.

♣ When I made up my spray on the pole it had more of a gracefully curving arch to it. It had to be flattened slightly to be photographed successfully (keeping the flowers large enough to be seen and the whole wedding cake on the page!)

♣ To set up the cake, place the back pole in position, then place the perspex stand in position. Arrange the cakes on the stand at an attractive angle. Position the central spray in place linking the two cakes together and linking trails from the pole to trails from the central spray. Set the smaller spray to the side of the cake.

♣ To transport the cake you will need to fasten the pole to a piece of pegboard with wires bound through the flowers, fastening the base to the pegboard.

Paste
*Pale melon, pale green,
mid green*

•

Cutters
*Periwinkle, (459) simple
leaf (226, 227, 228,
229, 230, 2331, 232)*

•

Stamens
Single yellow

•

Wire
28-gauge, 26-gauge

•

Tape
Nile green

•

Dusts
*White, primrose yellow,
lemon yellow, cornflower
blue, violet, plum, dark
green mixture, jade, lime
green, champagne*

PERIWINKLE

BUD

❧ Take a small piece of pale melon paste and form into a slender tube, thickening to a point at one end. Moisten the tip of a 28-gauge wire and insert it as far as possible into the bud.

❧ Make a cage with five 28-gauge wires. Insert the tip of the bud into the cage. Hold the wires, evenly spaced, above and below the bud and pull strongly.

❧ Gently pinch out each protruding piece of paste until it is very fine. Remove the cage and spiral the petals of the bud around one another tightly. Re-form the tip of the bud if distorted. Dust the bud, remembering to keep the pale melon showing from about half way down.

❧ To make the calyx, cut a very finely rolled pale green piece of paste into a square. Cut out long, slender wedges from the square, leaving five very delicate pointed sepals. Moisten the wire just below the bud and fasten the calyx in place. Dust with a little green from the base upwards while the calyx is still flexible. Dust the wire as well.

FLOWER

❧ Take a medium ball of melon paste and roll it into a teardrop. Roll the narrow end to make a fine tube. Flatten the broad end, place on the board, roll out finely and cut out the shape with the appropriate cutter. Remove the flower from the cutter and spread the petals on the board once again, tube upright. With one of the thicker celsticks, roll out the petals to a slight point. Turn the flower slightly on its side so that you can work on the right side of the petals. With a cocktail stick (toothpick), soften and subtly frill the edges.

❧ Open the throat of the flower slightly with a celstick. Using a five-pronged throat veining tool, open the throat properly. Gently insert the celstick so the ridges of paste are pushed backwards out of the centre. The points should go to the centre of each petal. With a flat-ended pair of tweezers, gently pinch in a ridge on the inside of the flower from point to point.

❧ Moisten the tip of a 26-gauge wire and insert it into the flower. Cut a stamen short and, after dusting the inside of the throat carefully with some yellow dust, add the stamen. Tweak the petals into place and allow to firm up.

❧ When set but not brittle, dust the petals from the edge inwards so that the dark colour remains on the edge and fades towards the centre. The pinched ridge is dusted white. Make the calyx as for the bud, using pale green paste.

LEAVES

❧ Roll out the mid green paste finely on a grooved board or with the grooved rolling pin. Cut out and gently soften the edge of the leaves. Moisten the tip of a 28-gauge wire for the smaller leaves and 26-gauge for the larger ones. Set aside to dry. Twist some gently into interesting shapes, and leave others with just a gentle curve.

Paste
*Pale melon, pale green,
mid green*

•

Cutters
*Briar rose petal (R14),
suitable calyx cutter
(R11)*

•

Stamens
*Roll of 120-gauge white
lacemakers' cotton thread*

•

Wire
*28-gauge white,
24-gauge wire*

•

Tape
Nile green

•

Dusts
*Brown, dark green, moss
green, silver lustre,
white, fuchsia pink,
primrose, lemon*

To make a half-open rose, use one layer of five petals with the top of the petals cut to a heart shape, worked fine, and then arranged around a tightly formed stamen centre. For a half-open flower, there would be no brown on the stamens at all. Dust them with primrose yellow. Add the calyx as described. This flower looks very good if it has been lightly steamed.

BRIAR ROSE

♣ To make the stamens, put a small celstick next to your finger. Bind the lacemakers' thread around it until you feel you have sufficient stamens for your flower. (It is important that the thread be cotton. Polyester cotton will not accept egg white and petal dust sufficiently.) Remove from your finger. Twist the thread into a figure of eight. Slip a piece of 28-gauge wire through both loops to secure it. Flatten the figure of eight, pulling it slightly off centre so one loop is larger than the other. Work the smaller loop inside the larger loop, twisting the wires together strongly. Cut through the thread with a pair of sharp scissors. Using your thumb as a template, cut around the top of the threads in a slight curve.

♣ Using ¼-width green tape, tape over the twisted wires. Carefully catching the base of the threads, tape around here as well, thus centralizing the 'stamens'. You should find that having tucked the shorter loop inside the longer loop there are short pieces of thread in the centre.

♣ Fluff out the threads slightly with a scriber. Dip the threads into egg white. Blot slightly on a piece of kitchen paper. Spread the threads with the scriber. With a pair of tweezers, curve the wet cotton into curves. Allow to dry. Fluff out the stamens with the scriber. The threads will remain curved.

♣ Take a tiny piece of pale green paste and roll it into a ball. Position it on your scriber. Very gently moisten it with egg white and stick into the centre of the stamens. With the scriber,

cut through the paste between the threads to fasten it firmly in place. Dust with a little green dust. With an emery board, gently roughen the tips of the thread.

♣ Paint a little moistened mixture of primrose and lemon on to the stamens and dip into a little yellowy/brown dust. If you are making a fully open rose where the stamens are all likely to be brown, gently singeing the threads with a nightlight gives a very realistic effect.

♣ Roll out the pale melon paste on a grooved board. Cut out five petals. Insert a moistened 28-gauge wire into the ridge at the tip of each petal. Using a finger, press out any ridges you do not need on the petal.

♣ Soften the edges of the petals with a ball tool on a pad of foam. With a pair of curved scissors, cut a heart shape into the petals. Once again soften the cut edge. With a large ball tool, work on the petals, cupping and curving them. Using a veining tool, add a bit more interest.

♣ Using a small celstick or cocktail stick, gently shape the petals. Set them on dimpled foam to firm up. When firm but not brittle, gently dust the petals. They should be yellow/gold near the tip, and a delightful pale pink near the edges.

♣ Tape the five petals around the prepared stamens, making sure that the last of the five petals is placed on top of the other petals and is not spiralled in a circle.

♣ Make a calyx as described for the rose. Decide whether or not to cut the slits on the sepals.

♣ To make a bud, use the first layer of the All-in-One Rose (see page 44).

HONEYSUCKLE

Paste
Pale melon, pale green

•

Cutters
*Honeysuckle
(HS 1, 2, 3)*

•

Stamens
*Miniature white or
yellow, small white or
pale green stamens for
pistil*

•

Wire
*28-gauge, cut into
quarters*

•

Tape
Nile green

•

Dusts
*Lemon yellow, primrose
yellow, apricot, pink,
plum, skintone, dark
green mixture*

•

*Note: Use simple leaf
cutters if you are making
fly honeysuckle, Japanese
honeysuckle or black
berried honeysuckle, side
petal of the slipper orchid
if you are making
perfoliate honeysuckle,
bougainvillaea cutters if
you are making common
honeysuckle.*

♣ Use one small white or pale green stamen as the pistil. This should be ¾-length. If using a white stamen, dust it a pale green. For the stamens use five heads of miniature white or yellow stamens at ½-length. Dust them with skintone dust. Fasten the pistil and stamens to a wire with ¼-tape or with a glue gun.

♣ To make the leaves, use the cutter that goes with the type of honeysuckle you have chosen. Unless you are using the simple leaf cutters, you will have to cut some leaves freehand to match the shape you have chosen, as there is not a wide selection of cutters available in the other shapes. Roll out the pale green paste fairly finely using either a grooved board or a grooved rolling pin. Cut out the leaf shapes required. Moisten the end of a wire and insert it into the central vein. Soften the edge of the leaves and use a home-made veiner or any that is close to the veining on the leaf of your chosen flower.

♣ When the leaves are firm but not brittle, dust them with the dark green dust. The leaves of the common honeysuckle and the Japanese honeysuckle tend to have a fine plum edge. When they are completely dry, dip them in a ½-glaze and when it is almost dry, scratch out the paler central vein.

♣ For the flower, make a tube with pale melon paste, flatten the broad end of the tube and roll it out finely on a non-stick board. Position the petal cutter over the tube and cut out the flower, smoothing off any rough paste on the heel of your hand. Remove the paste from the cutter and make a hole in the tube using a celstick, satay stick or skewer. Gently soften the edges of the petals. Using your veining tool, gently mark a line down the length of the long, slender petal. Curve this petal backwards strongly. Using a dresden tool, shape the petal which divides into the four smaller petals. Now curve these petals backwards as well.

♣ Moisten the wire just below the stamens and pistil and then gently curve them. Position them

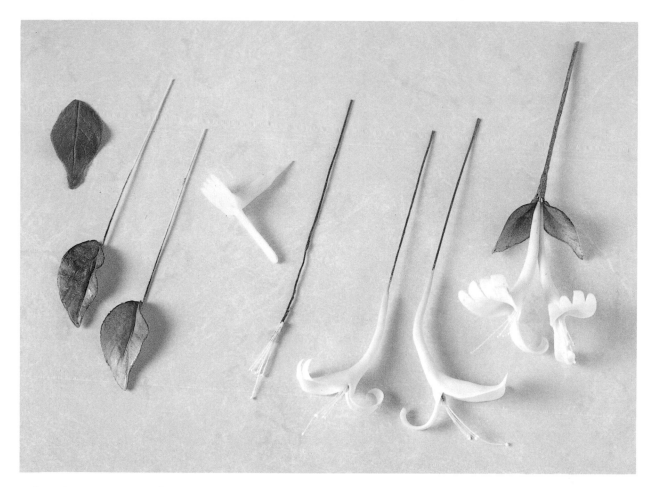

so that the stamens curl up towards the four small petals. Very gently curve the tube slightly. If you have time you can add a very tiny calyx to each flower. If not, you can create the impression of a calyx by dusting the base of the flower where it joins the wire with green petal dust.

♣ The buds are long narrow tubes with a slightly bulbous tip. Some are slightly curved like a lazy S, and others like a lazy C. It is best to make just one variety or they become difficult to arrange.

♣ Fly honeysuckle (despite its name it has a pretty flower, the pale cream petals darkening to a rich cream as the flower gets older) is arranged in short twigs branching off in pairs off the major stem. It is usual for the

twig to consist of a small pair of opposite leaves, and then with each succeeding pair of opposite leaves there is a long stalk ending in a pair of buds or flowers, backed by a pair of small bracts arising from the apex of each leaf (i.e. for every two leaves there are four flowers).

♣ The Japanese honeysuckle, although very similar to the fly honeysuckle, has the flowers arranged on shorter stems, and instead of just small bracts, they are backed by a pair of small leaves. This honeysuckle is a rich plummy pink.

♣ The stems of common honeysuckle tend to twine around one another, which gives a most attractive effect. They are a rich plum on the upper edge and green below (as are the stems of Japanese honeysuckle).

For long, loose sprays it is most attractive to make either the fly or Japanese honeysuckle. For others, where people may not recognize these less common honeysuckles, it is better to make the common honeysuckle clusters.

BITTERSWEET

Paste
*Pale melon, pale green,
mid green, egg yellow*

•

Cutters
*Calyx (R13), smallest
blossom plunger, simple
leaf (227–232)
bittersweet (577–579)*

•

Veiners
Deadly nightshade veiner

•

Stamens
*Miniature white stamen
off-cut*

•

Wire
*28-gauge, 26-gauge,
30- or 32-gauge white*

•

Tape
Nile green

•

Dusts
*Burgundy mixture, dark
green mixture, plum,
purple, cornflower blue,
egg yellow, lemon
yellow, apple, moss and
vine green, white dust or
paste colour, nasturtium,
black icing pen*

For buds, take a
piece of pale melon
paste, add a tiny
calyx on to the back
of the barrel before
pulling through an
unhooked 28-gauge
wire. Mark with a
cage made with five
30- or 32-gauge
wires. Dust a purply
mauve. Steam.

♣ Take a tiny ball of egg yellow paste. Moisten the tip of a 28-gauge wire and insert it. Turn the ball into a tiny carrot shape. Insert part of a miniature stamen off-cut into the front of the carrot of paste, leaving about 5–8 mm ($\frac{1}{4}$–$\frac{1}{3}$ inch) protruding from the front of the piece of paste. Using a craft knife, mark five indentations vertically around the piece of yellow paste. Dust with a mixture of lemon and egg yellow.

♣ Roll out a piece of the pale melon paste. Make a very small protrusion and roll out the paste very thinly. Cut out the shape. Place the cut-out piece on a foam pad with the small hip in the small hole. Soften the edges of the petals with a dog bone tool and then vein down the centre of each petal with your veining tool. Cut out a small blossom shape with the blossom plunger cutter and attach it to the small protrusion with a little egg white. Open the centre of the flower slightly with a celstick. Turn the petals front side down on the foam pad and stroke each petal gently with a dog bone tool so they curl backwards. (Try not to remove all of the central vein.)

♣ Moisten the back of the yellow anther, insert the wire through the centre of the petal shape and the calyx, and fasten it in place. Dust the petals with the burgundy dust and a bit of plum and cornflower blue if it is needed. Leave a ring of the pale melon around the yellow anther. Paint two small dots of white paste colour or moistened petal dust at the base of each petal alongside the anther. Using the icing pen, encircle the white paint with a black ring and reinforce the darker colour down the central veins in the petals. The flower should be steamed.

♣ These flowers grow in clusters of about fifteen blossoms and buds. The clusters are made up of smaller bunches of between two and five buds and flowers.

Berries: Make them egg-shaped. They have a calyx attached to them as for the flower and the bud, and range in colour from pale green through orange to fully ripe red berries. Dust with different combinations of the colours so they look natural. Glaze them with a $\frac{3}{4}$-to-full glaze.

Leaves: Roll out pale green paste using a grooved rolling pin or grooved board. Cut out the leaves. For the small leaves insert a moistened 28-gauge wire and for the larger leaves insert a moistened 26-gauge wire. Soften the edges gently on a foam pad. Vein them with the veiner and then place the veined leaf back on the foam pad. Using a dog bone tool, run firmly down the edge of each leaf so they ripple. Pinch in the main vein again to emphasize it and place it on dimpled foam to dry.

♣ When firm but not brittle, dust the leaves with purple at the edges, then go over the centre of each leaf with the dark green mixture and finally dust over the whole thing with moss green to blend all the colours together. Glaze the leaves with a $\frac{1}{2}$-glaze. Then, using a craft knife, scrape through to the light colour to show the veins.

BLACK BRYONY

Paste
Dark green, red

•

Cutters
Heart leaf (538, 539, 540)

•

Wire
28-gauge green, 20-gauge

•

Tape
Dark green

•

Dusts
Dark green mixture, red, black

♣ Roll out the paste on a grooved board, or using a grooved rolling pin. Roll out the front of the piece of paste, this will be where the tip of the leaf is positioned. Cut out the leaf, extend the paste into the curve of the leaf so it is almost, but not quite, straight.

♣ Insert a ¼-length wire quite a distance into the paste. Place on a foam pad and using a veining tool press veins into the paste following the line of the outer edge of the leaf. Pinch the tip of the leaf firmly between your finger and thumb, this gathers the tip together a little. When the leaf is leather hard, dust the leaf with the dark green dust. Glaze with a ¾ glaze.

BERRIES

♣ Make some small red balls, pull finely hooked 28-gauge wires through the upper surface of the ball and leave the hook buried in the ball. By pulling the hooked wire through the upper surface you have made a hole in the berry. Dust this with a little black dust. Dust the berries with the red dust and glaze with a full glaze.

♣ Tape the leaves on to a long 20-gauge wire, starting at the tip with some small leaves. They are taped on alternately leaving a long stalk going from the stem to the leaf. At the apex of some of the leaves tape in a cluster of about three berries. Curve the leaf stalks gracefully.

VARIEGATED IVY

Paste
Pale melon, dark green, mid green, pale green

•

Cutters
Large ivy cutters, variegator

•

Veiner
Ivy veiner

•

Wire
28-gauge, 26-gauge, 20-gauge

♣ Roll out some pale melon paste to a medium thickness. Roll equal amounts of pale melon and the three green pastes into sausages. Put the sausages alongside one another and roll into a long sausage. Twist the sausage, fold it in half and roll it into a sausage again. Repeat. Cut a thin slice off the end of the sausage and roll it wafer thin. The colours should be very mixed.

♣ Lift the variegated flat piece of paste and place it on the rolled out pale melon paste. Position on a grooved board and roll out together thinly. They should become one, leaving variegated markings.

♣ Using one of the large ivy cutters, cut out a leaf and soften the edge with a dog bone tool on a foam pad. Moisten a ¼ wire length, insert it into the central vein and then vein the leaf. Pinch the leaf forwards, reinforcing the central vein. Set it aside to dry. Glaze with a ½ glaze.

♣ Tape the variegated leaves on to a central wire as birdsfoot ivy. Prepare more leaves in the same way, using 26-gauge for the largest leaves, 28-gauge for medium and smaller leaves.

DARK IVY

♣ This is made in the same way as the birdsfoot ivy, but using the cutters (without the variegator) used for variegated ivy. Remember to dust, glaze and scrape out the pale veins. Wire together as described for birdsfoot ivy.

BIRDSFOOT IVY

Paste
Pale green

•

Cutters
German ivy, birdsfoot ivy (580–582)

•

Veiner
Ivy veiner

•

Wire
28-gauge, 26-gauge, 24-gauge, 20-gauge

•

Tape
Green, brown

•

Dust
Dark green mixture

♣ Roll out paste thinly using a grooved board or grooved rolling pin. Cut out the leaves. Soften the edges on a foam pad with a dog bone tool.

♣ Cut wires into quarters. Use 28-gauge wires for the small leaves and 26-gauge wires for the larger leaves. Moisten the tip of a wire and insert it into the central vein. Vein the leaf on a rubber veiner. Pinch the leaf from the back to reinforce the central vein. Set the leaf aside to harden on dimpled foam, which will give extra shaping to the leaf.

♣ When the leaf is firm but not brittle, dust it with the dark green dust mixture. Set it aside to harden completely. When it is dry, dip into a ½-glaze, set aside on kitchen paper to dry slightly and then, with a sharp craft knife, scrape away some of the dust and glaze to expose pale veins.

♣ Using ¼-width brown tape and a 24-gauge wire for a short stem of leaves, start taping, leaving about 2.5 cm (1 inch) tape loose above the wire. Twiddle this into a tendril. Starting with small leaves, tape them on to the central wire with brown tape. The stems of the leaves should be about 2.5 cm (1 inch) long. Tape them on alternately. Tape together different numbers of leaves on to stems, keeping to odd numbers. Twine the tendril around a small celstick to give it some movement. With a pair of tweezers or small pliers, lift each leaf and bend it so that it points outwards. All the leaves should be arranged over the central wire, slightly off to the side each time. Once all are in place, gently zig-zag the wire in between.

17

*Celcakes tilted perspex
separating stand, 12 cm
(4½ inch) high at the back
on a 13 cm (5 inch) base
18 cm (7 inch) and 28 cm
(11 inch) ellipse cake
23 cm (9 inch) and 36 cm
(14 inch) ellipse cake
board
White sugarpaste
White royal icing
No. 0 Bekenal tube
No. 00 Bekenal tube
Piped floral lace pieces
White picot-edged
ribbon for board edge*

•

FOR THE SPRAYS
*Florist's frog, Florist's
strip paste, White
600 ml yoghurt pot lid
(1 pint) Florist's oasis,
Medium dry oasis ball,
Binding tape*

For the Small Spray
*2 trails of birdsfoot ivy
(see page 17),
1 trail of variegated ivy
(see page 16),
1 white rose bud,
1 white half-rose,
1 spray of greeny white
dendrobium orchids*

For the Main Spray
*3 sprays of dark green
ruscus,
12 trails of birdsfoot ivy,
5 trails of variegated ivy,
5 sprays of stephanotis,
9 white rosebuds,
12 white half rosebuds,
9 white full roses,
7 longiflorum lilies,
3 longiflorum buds,
5 sprays of dendrobium
orchids*

White Beauty
WEDDING CAKE

This cake needs a stand made specially by Celcakes. I designed this one for my daughter Maggie's wedding. The base stand is 38 × 28 cm (15 × 11 inch) maximum.

♣ Cover the cakes and boards with white sugarpaste. Cut templates from the cake tins used. Place the templates on the boards where the cakes will be positioned, then remove the sugarpaste from this section. Crimp the edges of the board with a crimper. Leave to dry.

♣ Place the cakes on the boards, then pipe a fine snailtrail around the base of the cake. Attach the ribbon to the board. Mark the slanting lines for the lace on to the cake using a template. Make another template and transfer the lines of the piped heart on to the front of the small cake (see page 141 for lace template).

♣ Pipe the lace pieces, allowing approximately one third extra for breakages. This is very delicate. Pipe the embroidery on to the front of the small cake. Stick the lace in place on both cakes.

♣ Wire up the small spray into an attractive shape.

♣ Fasten the frog into the white yoghurt pot lid using florist's strip paste. Push the frog into the dry oasis ball, and fasten all this to the perspex disk at the top of the perspex arch using strong florist's binding tape. (The yoghurt pot lid prevents tiny pieces from the dried oasis ball falling on to the cake.)

♣ Starting with the foliage, arrange the spray as you would a flower arrangement. Remember that these flowers are more fragile than the real thing.

♣ To assemble the cake, transport the main spray *in situ*, or arrange it when you get to the wedding reception. The perspex base board can be fastened to a piece of pegboard with wires. The cakes travel in cake boxes, with the small spray separate.

♣ Once you have the cake stand on the table, place the large cake in its position. Stick a strip of double-sided tape to the top slanting piece of the separating stand, remove the top piece of paper and stick the small cake to the stand. Position it carefully before sticking the cake to the tape, as it is very difficult to move if it is in the wrong place.

♣ Put the small cake plus stand on to the large cake, being careful to avoid the delicate lace pieces. Fit this through from the back of the arrangement to avoid the long sprays of ruscus, ivy and the longiflorum lily and bud. Remember there is very delicate lace on the top tier as well. The pieces on the front of the cake on either side of the embroidery are particularly at risk at this stage. Place the small spray to the side of the cake stand, to complete the work.

STEPHANOTIS
(*Madagascan Jasmine*)

Paste
White, mid green

•

Cutters
*Stephanotis (566), small
(406) calyx*

•

Wire
26-gauge, 28-gauge

•

Dusts
*Champagne, apple
green, vine green*

✿ Roll white paste into a medium-sized ball, make a tube and pinch out the paste at the end. Roll out finely. Place the stephanotis cutter over the tube and cut out the flower. Invert the flower on to a foam pad. Soften the edge of the petals very gently with a dog bone tool. Stroke down the centre of the petals from the tube to the tip with a dresden tool (this makes the petals roll gently backwards). Open the throat of the flower with a celstick. Insert a moistened 26-gauge wire.

✿ Narrow down the paste immediately behind the petals by rotating the flower between your two forefingers. This should be about a third of the length of the tube. Flatten the base of the tube so that it is broader than the neck of the flower immediately behind the petals. Holding the petals against your finger, gently indent the front of the petal with the dresden tool, angling it across the centre of the throat. Very gently stroke up the tube with your fingers, pulling the petals upwards so they are not quite flat. Sometimes the petals do droop downwards, but this tends to make the flower look as though it needs water.

✿ Dust the tube of the flower with a little champagne dust, and

DECORATIVE TOUCHES

20

the lower section with apple and vine green mixed together.

♣ Roll out mid green paste very finely. Cut out the calyx. Moisten the base of the flower and thread the calyx into place, positioning the sepals so they fit between the petals at the top of the tube. The calyx is flat against the base, not curving upwards around the tube.

♣ These flowers look best steamed to give them a waxy look.

BUD

♣ Roll white paste into a thick tube. Insert a 26-gauge wire. Leave a thickened tip to the bud, with a point at the very end.

Narrow the paste behind what will be the head of the bud, as you did for the flower. The base of the bud is flattened as was the base of the flower. Attach a calyx as for the flower.

♣ Make a cage with five 28-gauge wires. Insert the tip of the bud into the cage and tighten to mark the indentations. Pinch slight ridges into the pieces of paste emerging between the wires. Dust the bud as for the flower, but using the green dust higher up the tube. Steam as for the flower.

♣ These flowers and buds grow in clusters, but florist's wire them up separately in sprays and bouquets.

Paste
White, pale green, mid green

•

Cutters
Rose petal (278, 277, 276, 551), calyx (R11), black plastic rose leaves

•

Veiners
Briar rose leaf veiner

•

Wire
20-gauge, 24-gauge, 28-gauge green

•

Tape
Nile green

•

Dusts
White, primrose yellow, vine green, moss green, silver lustre, apple green, jade, fuchsia pink, red

ROSE

♣ First make the central knob. To decide the size, it should fit inside the cutter selected for the inner petals. Take a ball of white paste, roll it into a cone shape with a rounded base and a sharp point. Hook a 20-gauge wire, and then either moisten it with egg white or heat it until it is red hot and insert it into the paste. Be careful not to get melted sugar on your hands.)

♣ Roll out a piece of white paste very thinly. Cut out as many petals as you can, using the cutter selected for the inner petals. This will be the smallest cutter used for the rose. Keeping one petal out, tuck the others between the sheets of a celflap or inside a plastic folder to keep them moist.

♣ *Layer 1*: Place the petal on a foam pad, soften the edge carefully with the large end of a dog bone tool. It is important that the tool be half on the petal and

half on the pad. Moisten the petal, place the central knob against the petal, allowing the petal to protrude 5 mm ($\frac{1}{4}$ inch) or more above the tip of the knob. Roll the petal around the knob, making sure it is tightly wrapped at the tip. You should not be able to see the knob at all through the top of the petal.

♣ To turn this into a bud, roll back the edge of the petal right down to the base and add a calyx.

♣ *Calyx*: Roll a small piece of pale green paste flat. Take a piece of mid green paste, form a short tube with it and flatten the broad end of the tube. Press this flattened piece of paste against the rolled out piece of paste. Roll out both layers of paste at the same time on a Mexican hat board. When the paste is fairly thin, cut out the calyx. Elongate each sepal. Run the dresden tool then the veining tool down the centre of each, cut the serrations at the side of the sepals. There is an old country saying which describes

these serrations: 'Two with two and two without, one with one and one without'. The last line belonging to just one sepal. Using a dog bone tool, run it from the tip of the sepals to the centre, curling them up.

♣ When adding the calyx to a bud, hollow the calyx in the centre. Dust the inside of the calyx with a little silver lustre. Insert the wire from the rose through the moistened centre of the calyx and down through the hip. Be careful to fasten one of the uncut sepals over the join. The next sepal to be put in place is the other sepal with no cuts, followed by the one with the notch on one side and then finally the two sepals that each have two cuts on either side. A calyx can be added to a bud as soon as it is made. If you are making a rose, not just a bud, continue from here, adding the calyx at the end.

♣ *Layer 2*: Take three petals and soften the edges on the pad of foam, remembering to keep the dog bone tool half on the petal and half on the foam pad. Work the surface of the petals slightly so they are a little larger than the petal surrounding the central knob. Moisten the point and the left-hand side of each petal with a little egg white. Stick the left-hand edge of one petal to the central knob with the join from the first layer arranged at the centre of this first petal. Join the left edge of the other two petals to the knob as well, spacing them evenly around the centre. This layer should be fractionally taller than the central petal.

♣ To give the rose a tight centre, pull gently down on the right-hand edge of each petal, not so hard that they end up lower than the central layer, but enough to create a tight centre. Gently unfurl a fraction of each of these three petals to give a natural look.

♣ To turn this into a bud, curl back the petals down the edges and add a calyx, noting the order of sticking the sepals in place.

♣ *Layer 3*: Repeat as for Layer 2, but do not fasten the petals down quite so tightly. These petals should also be enlarged by working them a little. Unfurl a little more of each of these petals. Once again these petals should be fractionally taller than the previous layer. The joins of the petals from the previous layer should each go to the centre of the petals in the next layer.

♣ *Layer 4*: Cut another three petals, soften the edges as before and enlarge them slightly. With a large ball tool, cup the three petals. Moisten the tip of each of these petals. Attach as before, positioning the joins of the previous layer to the centre of each of these petals. The petals once again should be fractionally taller than those of the previous three layers and this layer should also be spiralled. Stick just the lower sides and edges of the petals to the rose and do not flatten the cupping when adding the petals.

♣ Curl back the side edges of these petals strongly. The sides of two of the petals should be curled back so far that the previous petals are exposed right down to the base.

♣ At this stage, you have a half-rose, which is frequently used in sprays. Add a calyx.

♣ *Layer 5*: For this layer the size of the cutter is increased. Roll out a further piece of white paste very thinly and cut out 5 petals. Soften the edges of the petals and cup them with the large ball tool. Moisten the tip and side edges of

the petals. The first petal should be fastened carefully in place across the front of the rose. Be careful not to flatten the cupping. Move across the rose to the opposite side and attach a petal over the join. Using a cocktail stick, roll the top edges and sides of the petals into attractive shapes. These petals should be the same height as the previous layer. Continue adding the petals to this layer, moving from one side to the other so you get some movement to the rose. Curl back the tops and the sides of these petals so they look natural.

♣ *Layer 6*: Using the slightly larger cutter, cut out another five petals. Soften the edges and cup them strongly. With a cocktail stick, curl the top and sides of the petals before sticking them in place on the rose. Once again move backwards and forwards across the rose. In each place, the petal should be fastened over the joint of a previous layer. Roll the sides of some of these petals so far back that they are almost falling off the rose.

♣ Before the rose is too dry, dust the base of the petals with a little primrose and vine green. Steam the rose. Dust it yet again. Now you may add the calyx. *Note*: The calyx on a full blown

rose should curl back completely. One thing to bear in mind is that you should not add the calyces to roses which are to be wired into a spray until the last minute. This ensures that the sepals will be damp and will not break off as easily during the wiring process.

LEAVES

♣ Roll two balls of paste, a larger one of mid green and another of pale green. Squash them together and roll out the paste either on a grooved board or with a grooved rolling pin.

♣ Cut out the leaves. A normal garden rose tends to have a compound leaf containing five leaflets – one large one, two slightly smaller and two smaller still. Briar or dog roses tend to have compound leaves with between seven and eleven leaflets, which are all approximately the same size. Hybrid roses sometimes only have three leaflets in a compound leaf. Soften the edge of each leaf with a dog bone tool on a foam pad. Moisten the tips of $\frac{1}{4}$-length pieces of 28-gauge wire and insert one into each leaf. Shape the leaves with your fingers. Vein the leaves. Set aside to firm up.

♣ Dust the leaves using a combination of dark green mixture, apple green, moss green, jade, fuchsia pink and red. Some varieties of leaves have only a little red on them, others a lot. Remember to keep the underside of the leaves paler than the upper surface.

♣ Glaze the leaves with a $\frac{1}{2}$-glaze.

Make the compound rose leaves and wire the leaves, buds and flowers together to form an attractive informal spray.

DENDROBIUM ORCHID

Paste
White

•

Cutters
Dendrobium (large 441, 442, 443), (small 486–489)

•

Veiners
Poppy petal veiner, corn-on-the-cob leaf veiner, or Hawthorn Hill veiner

•

Wire
24-gauge white

•

Tape
White

•

Dusts
Vine green, primrose, lemon yellow

♣ *Column*: Take a small piece of white paste. Form it into a teardrop shape. Measure the cutter from the squared back of the tongue cutter to the top of the two side protrusions. The column should not be longer than this measurement. Curve the teardrop, hollow the inside curve gently.

♣ Make a hook at one end of a $\frac{1}{3}$-length of 24-gauge wire. Moisten the hook with egg white. Pull the wire through the curved column to between a half and a third of the length of the column, closer to the pointed end than to the broad end. Bury the hook in the paste at the broad end of the teardrop. Gently flatten the broad end of the column. Add a tiny ball of paste to this front flattened lip and then gently split it into two with the blade of your craft knife to form the pollinia. Gently pinch a ridge along the spine of the column. Set it aside to dry completely.

♣ *Labellum:* Roll out a piece of white paste. Cut out one labellum shape. Soften the edges of the labellum. Stretch the paste of the two side protrusions forwards slightly, cupping them very gently at the same time. On some dendrobium orchids the tip of the labellum is pointed, on others it is fairly flat with a very small protrusion in the centre. Use a veining tool to vein strongly down the centre of the petal.

♣ Roll out another straight piece of paste, half the width of the central petal and to just past the junction of the two side protrusions. This piece of paste should be very strongly veined. Moisten the square back of the shape and the side of the two protrusions. Attach it to the tongue with a little egg white. The front lip of the tongue is recurved. The tongues of freshly opened flowers are not curved downwards, and the front sections of the lip are pinched upward as well. Tape over the wire with white tape to thicken it slightly. Set aside to dry completely.

♣ *Lateral Petals*: The lateral or side petal is a narrow, slightly pointed petal, with strong, almost parallel veining, which is strongest near the centre. Cut out two petals and soften the edges. Vein the petals with the veining tool. Set aside for a short while to firm up a little, curving the petals backwards slightly. It is easiest to curve them on either side of the corner of a foam pad so you get a slight slant to the curve.

♣ The style of lateral petals depends on the variety of dendrobium that is being made. The white bridal dendrobium has fairly straight lateral petals, but the more colourful dendrobium tends to have rounded, slightly fluted petals.

♣ *Sepals:* It is important to remember that this orchid has a spur at the back. To achieve this shape it is best to roll out the paste on a grooved board, having a thickened piece of paste between the lateral sepals. Cut out a shape, aiming the point between the lateral sepals straight up the thickened piece of paste. Gently soften the edges of the sepals. A little extra pressure can be used on the upper edges of the two lateral sepals; this will encourage

the sepals to curve in the right direction. Use the chosen veiner to create parallel veining on all three sepals. Using a veining tool, add extra, strong veins to the centre of the two lateral sepals. These sepals are often referred to as the 'legs', and to make people remember that these two sepals are to have strong veins, I usually refer to them as the 'varicose veins'! Pinch the tips of these two sepals forward.

♣ Place the shape on to a foam pad. Use the dresden foot of a veining tool to press firmly on to the thickened section of the back sepal, with the point of the tool aiming at the point which is situated between the two lateral sepals.

♣ Moisten the base of the two lateral petals and attach them to the sepals, fastening them securely in place at the junction of the dorsal and lateral sepals.

♣ Moisten the sepals from the base of the dorsal sepal to the point between the lateral sepals, extending outwards slightly along the lower edge of the lateral sepals. Pull wire through the sepals in the centre of the junction between the dorsal and lateral sepals. Make sure the dorsal sepal is attached to the column. In the real flower the column is an absolutely integral part of the dorsal sepal.

♣ Pinch the point between the lateral sepals firmly on to the spur created by the column. Pinch the lateral sepals forward. Recurve them, reinforcing the central vein. The dorsal sepal curves forward and inward towards the column at the base, but then curves backwards very strongly thereafter, retaining the concave shape of the sepal.

♣ Hang the orchid upside down to dry, so the petals and sepals fall into the correct positions. A former, made out of a tin can or aluminium foil, may help with this process.

♣ Newly opened flowers are almost completely very pale green, so dust lightly with vine green. The flowers open up from the bottom of the spike, so the lower flowers are more cream than green. Dust the dendrobium lightly with primrose and lemon yellow.

♣ There are approximately ten to fifteen flowers and buds on a spike. The stems of the orchid flowers are approximately 3.5–5 cm (1½–2 inch) and form a long flowing S-shape to join the spike.

♣ Each flower grows about 3 cm (1¼ inch) apart from those on either side of it; the flowers spiral evenly around the stem.

BUD

♣ The buds of the dendrobium vary between about 1–3 cm (½–1¼ inch) long. The larger they are the more they curve. The small buds at the tip of a spike are almost slipper-shaped, but the profile of the large buds are more bird-like in shape.

♣ To make the buds, take a piece of white paste and roll it into a teardrop shape. Pinch the tip to a sharp point and curve

it very slightly.

♣ The front of the bud is slightly rounded, but the whole thing curves backwards making a very shallow S-shape. The back of the bud is hollowed and a pointed tail is formed at the back. A 24-gauge wire, thickened with white tape, emerges about two-thirds of the way down the bud from the front, just about where the tail curves back at the rear of the bud. The wire is bent into a very shallow S-shape and can be anything from 2.5–3.5 cm (1–1½ inch) long.

♣ The smaller and newer the buds the greener they tend to be; dust with vine green, larger buds with primrose and lemon yellow.

♣ The buds have three lines of deeper colour showing where the sepals join together.

RUSCUS

Paste
Dark green

•

Cutters
Sepals of cattleya orchids (325, 8, 11)

•

Veiner
Poppy petal veiner

•

Wire
28-gauge, 20-gauge

•

Tape
Dark green

•

Dusts
Dark green mixture

♣ Roll out the paste using a grooved rolling pin or a grooved board. Cut out the leaves and soften the edges without fluting them.

♣ Moisten the tip of a 28-gauge wire, cut into quarters, and insert into the central vein of each leaf. Add some texture with the poppy petal veiner.

♣ Dust the upper surface of the leaves with the dark green mixture. Curve each leaf gently across its width and set aside to dry.

♣ When the ruscus leaves are dry glaze them with a ¾-glaze. Tape the leaves on to 20-gauge wire; start with one leaf and spiral them down the length of the stalk.

LONGIFLORUM LILY

Paste
White, pale green

•

Cutters
Hawthorn Hill pistil former, Longiflorum

•

Veiner
Longiflorum (569, 570)

•

Stamens
Large lily

•

Wire
26-gauge white, 24-gauge green, 20-gauge

•

Tape
Nile green

•

Dusts
Apple green, vine green, primrose yellow, lemon yellow

♣ Dust the stamens with a mixture of lemon and primrose yellow.

♣ Make the pistil by rolling a pale green piece of paste on to a 24-gauge green wire. The paste should taper to nothing at the base and should be smooth and even to the tip. Roll out a small piece of green paste, press it into a pistil former. Moisten the tip of the paste-covered wire with a little egg white, touch it to the centre of the paste in the former and fasten in place. If you do not have a pistil former, you can shape the top of the pistil into a trefoil shape and mark a line down the centre of each protrusion. The pistil should be about two-thirds of the length of a petal. Dust the pistil with apple green. When it is dry, glaze it with a full glaze.

♣ To make the flower, roll out white paste on a grooved board. Cut out the petals and with the larger cutter imbed a 26-gauge white wire in each petal as far as it will go. Place the petals on a foam pad and gently soften the edges. Place in the veiner and press gently but firmly. Remove from the veiner and curl the upper side edges of the petals inward. Allow to dry with the petals supported in a slight curve and the tip curving backwards as well. When the three larger petals are firm but not brittle, tape them together around the pistil and six stamens, which are joined just below the pistil.

♣ Cut out three petals with the narrower cutter on the grooved board (these petals are not wired but there is a ridge on the rear of each). Press the petals in the veiner. Shape the tip of the petals as before, but on this occasion the petals curl back more strongly than the inner layer. One at a time fasten these petals to the inner ones, lining up the lower edge precisely. Do not try to attach petals that have become too dry or struggle to attach them all at once.

♣ Dust the lilies with a little vine and apple green mixed into cornflour. This will stop the petals becoming green too fast. I usually lighten petal dust with white petal dust, but it tends to go streaky on so large an area. The younger and fresher the flower, the greener the tone.

BUD

♣ Use a 20-gauge wire taped with green tape. Hook the wire and moisten the end. Insert into a large sausage of white paste. Work the paste on to the wire very firmly. Create a graceful curve to the tip of the bud.

♣ Tape six 24-gauge wires together to form a cage. Space the wires so that you have two close together, then a gap, then two close together, then a gap, etc. Put the bud point first into the cage. Gently close the cage, keeping the wires in three pairs. The paste between these pairs of wires is fatter than the piece of paste between the paired wires. Very gently pinch a ridge up the thickened protrusions of paste. Remove the cage. Dust the closely positioned veins with a mixture of apple and vine green, as well as the base of the bud. Allow to dry well.

♣ The longiflorum flowers and their buds all look better if they have been steamed.

Pink Rose and Gardenia
WEDDING CAKE

This cake has been designed using teardrop tins, which provide very little cake for eating. If more slices are needed, a cutting cake can be made for use at the wedding but kept out of sight in the kitchen.

20 cm (8 inch) and
25 cm (10 inch)
teardrop shaped cakes
25 cm (10 inch) and 30
cm (12 inch) oval cake
boards
Shell pink sugarpaste
White royal icing
Lace pieces
Pink ribbon to decorate
Crystal Wilton pillar
Offset perspex cake stand

•

FOR THE SPRAY
3 wired gardenias
(see page 32)
15 pink rosebuds
(see page 21 or 44)
5 pink half-roses
(see page 21 or 44)
Coffee flowers
Chinese jasmine flowers
Sprays of birdsfoot ivy

♣ Cover the cakes and boards with shell pink sugarpaste. Cut templates from the cake tins used. Place the templates on the boards where the cakes will be positioned, then remove the sugarpaste from this section. Crimp the edges neatly with a crimper. Leave to dry.

♣ When the sugarpaste is dry, fasten slightly darker pink ribbon around the base of each cake, finishing the join with a tiny bow. Pipe white snailtrail over the lower edge of the ribbon. Edge the board with picot-edged ribbon, the same colour as that used around the base of the cakes. Tie three bows with the narrow ribbon, leaving long tails. These will be taped on to the handle of the spray to hang down in an attractive manner.

♣ Pipe sufficient pieces of lace (see page 141) to fit the upper edge of the tiers, allowing a few extra for breakages.

♣ The cake has been designed to fit on an offset perspex stand. At the rear of the large tier, insert a crystal Wilton pillar to hold the spray.

♣ To make the spray you will need three wired gardenias (each with a bud and the surrounding corolla of leaves), fifteen pink rosebuds, five pink half-roses, coffee flowers for the intermediate flowers and pink-flushed Chinese jasmine flowers and buds to make the beginning of the trails. One very long, two medium and a good number of smaller ivy sprays make up the leaves for the backing. Start each trail with an ivy spray. Tape three of these together firmly to form the backbone of the spray. Gradually bring in ivy sprays between these, adding flowers where they are needed. The centre of the spray is made up with a cluster of gardenias and roses.

♣ It is usually safer to put the flowers on a cake before the lace, but in this case, where the spray of flowers is separate, the lace has to be attached to the cake before setting up. Great care must be taken not to break the lace pieces. The lace can be taken closer to the spray and finished with a little delicate embroidery, but I did not feel this was necessary when I was putting the cake together. I preferred to let the flowers speak for themselves.

WIRED GARDENIA

Paste
White, mid green, dark green

•

Cutters
Christmas rose, (282, 283, 284) simple leaf, broad side petal of a cattleya orchid, large hyacinth (303)

•

Veiners
Christmas rose petal, gardenia leaf

•

Stamens
Medium pale yellow (Most gardenias do not have stamens, so if you prefer you can leave them out.)

•

Wire
28-gauge white, 24-gauge white, 28-gauge green, 26-gauge green

•

Tape
White, mid green, dark green

•

Dusts
Dark green mixture, apple green, vine green

♣ **Method 1** *Layer 1*: For a gardenia without stamens, make a small cone of white paste as for a small rose (see page 21). Roll out a small piece of white paste and cut out six petals. Soften the edges. Pinch the tips and cup them gently. Moisten the left-hand edge of the petals and attach them to the cone, spiralling them neatly, making sure the cone is hidden once all six are in place.

♣ **Method 2** *Layer 1*: Fasten five pale yellow medium stamens to a 24-gauge white wire using white tape. Using a grooved rolling pin or grooved board, roll out some white paste finely, making a central vein. Cut out six petals, soften the edges with a dog bone tool, vein with a suitable sized veiner and insert a moistened white wire into each. Pinch the tip of each petal to a point. The petals surrounding the stamens are spiralled tightly into one another, so you have to form them into this shape while they are soft. Arrange them in a holder. It is wise to gently bind the wires together in place before putting them in a holder, so that they will remain in the same position while drying, and then when you pull the stamens into place. If you get the petals muddled it is quite difficult to get them to fit together once they have set.

♣ *The next two layers of petals are the same for both methods.*
Roll out more white paste on a grooved board or using a grooved rolling pin. Cut out six medium petals, soften the edges with a dog bone tool, cup them gently and vein with the Christmas rose veiner. Insert a

28-gauge white wire into the central vein. Using dimpled foam, support the petals in the position you want. It is not necessary to dry these petals slotted into one another, as at this second layer they are a little less cupped and shaped. Pinch the tips of the petals.

♣ Using the third sized cutter, make six more petals as before. They are not quite as cupped as the second layer. Dry on the dimpled foam.

♣ For the fourth layer, you do not have to use six petals, three is quite sufficient. They can be the same size as in the third layer, but if you want a little variation you can use a mixture of the two larger sizes. Cut them out, soften the edges, cup them deeply and then vein them. Set them aside to dry.

♣ To assemble the flower:
Method 1 Take your cone with its spiralled petals and gradually tape in (with white tape) the six petals from the next layer, spiralling them as well, making sure that the joins of the first layer of petals meet the centre of each petal of the next layer. Bind the petals in tightly. Add the third layer, centring these petals over the joins of the previous layer. Add a few petals to make up the fourth layer, but remember that these petals curve in the opposite direction from those of the previous three layers – they curve down.

♣ The gardenia has a short tube at the back. As these petals are wired to make arranging the flower easy, full-width white tape must be tightly bound behind the petals, to form the

tube. Immediately behind the flower a number of wires have been taped together and the stem would appear over-thick if you don't cut out a great many. This thinning can also make the petals less firm when you are arranging the flowers.

Method 2 Surround the cluster of stamens with the small petals, spiralling them at the same time. The other layers are the same as before.

❁ To make a calyx, roll out some mid green paste flat. Cut it out with the large hyacinth cutter. Using a medium celstick, elongate the sepals slightly and then broaden them a little. Now make a tube, fit the hyacinth

Each flower needs to be surrounded by a corolla of green leaves. You can omit these when wiring the flowers into a spray with other flowers and leaves, but I prefer to present them with their green corollas.

cutter over it and cut it out. Soften each sepal with the dog bone tool. Use the veiner to indent each sepal strongly so it folds in half. With the dog bone tool, make an indentation in the centre of the calyx with the tube. Lining the sepals in between the backing layer, gently attach the flat calyx. Moisten the centre slightly and thread the calyx on to the flower wire. Make sure the sepals are placed across the petal joins.

BUD

♣ The gardenia bud is simple to make. Make a cone of white or green paste (the smaller buds are very green in colour, almost the same colour as the small leaves). Moisten a hooked white or green wire and insert it into the cone. Form a slender tube below the bud.

♣ Make a cage using six 28-gauge wires. Insert the tip of the bud into the cage, spread the wires evenly and tighten the wires gently so they bite into the paste. Grasp the wires where they are joined and pull the wires in opposite directions. This makes them bite into the paste very deeply. While the wires are still being held firmly in place, pinch the bulges of paste into fine petals. Remove the wire and spiral the petals tightly together. The petals of the young green buds do not need to be pinched fine, but do need to be spiralled in the same way as the mature petals.

♣ Make a calyx as described for the flower and pull this behind the bud. This job is made easier if the bud has been allowed to dry first. For small green buds, there is no need to make the inner calyx as that is represented by the green

paste; you only need to add the narrow outer calyx with its short tube. In some cases the outer calyx is the same length as the height of the bud.

♣ Dust an almost mature bud and calyx with a mixture of the apple and vine greens, the outside of the outer calyx is a little darker. The buds lighten in colour as they get larger, being stark white when at the opening stage. At the same time the calyx gets smaller in proportion with the bud. The small green buds are also very shiny so need to be dipped in some full glaze after they have been dusted.

LEAVES

♣ Each gardenia flower or bud is surrounded by a collar of leaves. The smaller leaves, which generally grow around the bud, are a bright rather apple/lime green, the same sort of colour as the small green buds. The larger the leaves get, the darker they become.

♣ Roll out the dark green paste on a grooved board or with a grooved rolling pin. Cut out the leaves. Soften the edges on a foam pad with a dog bone tool, then vein them. Turn the leaf over so the underside is uppermost. Gently run the dog bone tool around the leaf inside the edge. This makes the edge of the leaf curve backwards slightly. Turn the leaf over and gently reinforce the central vein by pinching it in from the rear of the leaf. This reshapes the leaf.

♣ Dust larger, more mature leaves with the dark green mixture and gradually lighten the green as the leaves get smaller. If you want to be entirely accurate you should scrape in a light central vein after glazing the leaves with a full glaze.

CHINESE JASMINE

Paste
White, mid green

•

Cutter
Small stephanotis cutter

•

Stamens
*Medium pale yellow
hammerhead*

•

Wire
28-gauge green

•

Dusts
Pink, plum

♣ Make a very fine tube of white paste. Flatten the broad end and roll out very thinly, ensuring you don't get a wedge shape between the tube and the petal. Place the cutter over the tube and cut out a flower. Before removing the flower from the cutter, clean off any paste that may cause untidy edges.

♣ Place the flower on a foam pad and soften the edges of the petals with a dog bone tool. Moisten the tip of 28-gauge green wire and pull it through the centre of the flower. Carefully fasten the tube to the wire, tapering it. Cut off a short stamen and insert it into the centre of the flower, allowing it to protrude slightly.

♣ To make a calyx, roll out a small piece of mid green paste very finely. Cut a small square. Cut out long narrow wedges from one side, leaving five long

sepals. Moisten the wire just below the flower and attach the calyx at this point.

Bud: Roll a small ball of white paste into a very slender tube, thickening at one end. Make the thicker end into a sharp point. Moisten the tip of 28-gauge green wire and insert it into the tube. A short way from the sharp point at the thicker end of the tube, roll the paste on the wire firmly between your fingers, creating a fine neck. Make the rest of the tube behind this even finer, tapering it on to the wire. Make the calyx as for the flower (see above).

♣ Dust the bud pink along one side. Repeat this dusting on the flower, colouring only the back of one petal pink. Wire flowers and buds into clusters, curving the wires gently.

The flowers are very delicate with a very fine tube, so it is important to get this effect when making them.

Wiring of Waterfall Sprays

The picture on the left shows the components required to form a waterfall bridal bouquet.

The first pieces to fasten together are the upper and lower sprays. The upper spray forms a third of the length of the bouquet and the lower, two thirds. The gardenia which is the focal point, is slightly higher than the other flowers, and is at the centre of the bouquet, at the point where the two sprays meet. Do not wire in until outer sprays are in place.

The wires for each spray must be long enough to bend at a 90° angle and tape together to form the handle. Gradually incorporate all the pieces, removing excess wire. Check that the faces of the flowers are not hidden behind any foliage. The focal point, the main flower, is always positioned above the junction of the two major sprays.

Paste
White, pale green

•

Cutters
Large stephanotis (566), fine calyx (527). For leaves – simple leaf (227, 229, 226,) broad petal of cattleya orchid (9, 6)

•

Veiners
Poinsettia veiners in various sizes

•

Wire
26-gauge white and green, 18-gauge

•

Tape
White, brown

•

Dusts
Apricot, primrose yellow, moss green, apple green, vine green, jade, nutkin brown, black, red

COFFEE FLOWER

♣ Make the pistil by taping ¼-width white tape to 26-gauge wire, leaving 1 cm (½ inch) tape above the wire. Cut this tape in half lengthwise and curve the ends away from one another with a cocktail stick.

♣ Take a medium ball of white paste and roll it into a narrow tube at one end. Flatten the rest of the paste and roll it out fairly thinly on a non-stick board. Place the stephanotis cutter over the tube and cut out the flower. Clean off the jagged paste from the cutter and push the flower out of the cutter. Place the flower on a pad of foam. Soften the edge of each petal and then stroke the petals from the centre to the tip with a dresden tool. This will elongate the petals slightly and make the edges of the petals curl backwards. Open the throat of the flower with a celstick, gently pushing the petals upwards.

♣ With a very fine brush, dust the inside of the tube with a little apricot and primrose yellow dust, making sure that it does not spread on to the petals.

♣ Make the stamens by rolling out a piece of white paste fairly thinly. Cut out the calyx shape and remove from the cutter, having brushed off any rough pieces from the edge. Place this on to a foam pad. Run the veiner tool down the centre of each sepal from the tip to the centre. This makes them curl slightly.

♣ Moisten the inner edge of the tube of the flower with a little egg white, pick up the stamens using a celstick into the centre of the calyx shape and push this into the tube. Twist gently to loosen the stamens, making sure that the stamens are arranged between the petals of the flower. Now gently insert the wire with the pistil attached through the flower and arrange the pistil just above the stamens.

♣ Dust the base of the tube and the wire with a mid green dust, made by mixing moss and apple green.

COFFEE CHERRY
♣ This is the name given to the fruit which contains the coffee bean. On some plants these cherries grow in pairs from the apex of the paired leaves, and on others they grow in clusters. As coffee is a tropical product it tends not to be seasonal. The main flowering time is in March, but the plants produce new buds approximately fourteen days after heavy rainfall, so like citrus plants you will find buds, flowers and mature fruit all together on one plant at the same time.

♣ To make a cherry, take a ball of pale green paste and roll it into a barrel shape. Insert a hooked wire into the back, fasten securely to the wire and cut off cleanly at the base of the cherry. The tip of the cherry is slightly pointed, but this becomes flattened when you mark two small circles on to the tip using No. 2 and 3 piping tubes.

♣ Dust the cherries in a range of colours from pale green to a rich red. Naturally the green cherries are smaller than the ripe red ones. Once they are dry dip in a full glaze.

LEAVES
♣ Roll out the pale green paste fairly thinly, using a grooved board or a grooved rolling pin. Cut out the leaf shapes. Moisten 26-gauge wires and insert into the leaves. Soften the edges of the leaves on a foam pad with a dog bone tool. Vein the leaves using a poinsettia veiner and put them over shaped foam to give some movement to them.

♣ When the leaves are firm but not brittle, dust them. The smaller leaves are dusted with a little lime green, made by mixing vine green with a little apple green. As the leaves move up the stem they become larger and darker, so gradually dust the leaves with a deeper green until you reach the cattleya cutters. These leaves are dusted with a dark green dust. When the leaves are completely dry, dip them into a ½-glaze, and when dry, use a craft knife to scrape out a pale central vein down the leaf.

♣ The smaller leaves are bound into clusters in pairs and attached to an 18-gauge wire with brown tape, which also binds the wire. The larger leaves are opposites, spiralling down the stem.

Porcelaine
WEDDING CAKE

*30 cm (12 inch), 23 cm
(9 inch) and 15 cm
(6 inch) round cakes
40 cm (16 inch), 30 cm
(12 inch) and 23 cm
(9 inch) round cake
boards
Champagne sugarpaste
White royal icing
Ivory picot-edged
ribbon for board edges
1 Wilton flower pick
6 large celpicks for the
sides of the bottom and
middle tiers
3 small celpicks for the
sides of the top tier
Stacking perspex dividers
for separating the tiers*

This three-tier wedding cake is named after the porcelaine rose, a very popular flower for weddings. It is a comparatively large rose with a lovely neat bud.

♣ Cover the cakes and boards with champagne sugarpaste. Cut templates from the cake tins used. Place the templates on the boards where the cakes will be positioned, then remove the sugarpaste from this section. Crimp the edges of the board with a suitable crimper. Leave to dry.

♣ When the sugarpaste has set, position the cakes on their respective boards. Attach the ribbon around the edge of the boards. Divide the circumference of each cake into three, then mark the spot where the picks are to be inserted. Make small, deep holes into the sides of the cake before attempting to push the picks into place. This will prevent the sugarpaste from cracking around the picks. For this particular design the picks should be inserted about 1 cm ($\frac{1}{2}$ inch) from the board.

♣ Insert the Wilton flower pick into the centre of the top tier, once again taking the precaution of making a small, deep hole before attempting to push the whole pick into the cake. It is sensible to leave the picks protruding from the cake by about 5 mm ($\frac{1}{4}$ inch). This is to ensure that whoever cuts the cake will see the picks and remove them before the cake is sent out

to the guests.

♣ Pipe a fine shell border around the base of each cake where it is joined to the board.

♣ Wire up the various sprays. Arrange the ivy trails on the bottom tier so that they almost meet. Curve them gently away from one another. The third ivy trail should be encouraged to curve up on to the surface of the cake. In each case I like the sprays to be taller than the height of each tier. Make sure the stems you are creating are not too thick to fit into the picks. Have a loose pick to hand so that you can check the fit.

♣ The top spray is arranged to look good from any angle.

♣ If you are not going to assemble the cake yourself, it is a good idea to leave precise instructions on how to put the cake together, which way up and where the dividers are to be placed, which side of the tier is to be positioned to the front and so on. You cannot rely on other people to see the composition the way you do. Post-it notes are very good for this.

♣ It is unwise to allow people to divide the sprays into individual components as accidents with flowers containing wires are more likely to occur with a small item than with a large one.

Central spray for the top tier	3 side sprays for the top tier each consist of:	3 side sprays for the medium tier each consist of:	3 side sprays for bottom tier each consist of:
5 trails of dark ivy leaves (see page 16)	*1 trail of dark ivy leaves shorter than those used on the upper spray (see page 16)*	*3 trails of dark ivy leaves (see page 16)*	*3 large trails of dark ivy leaves (see page 16)*
3 sprays of freesias		*1 spray of freesias*	*3 sprays of freesias*
5 Java orchids	*3 sprigs of lily-of-the-valley*	*5 sprigs of lily-of-the-valley*	*3 Java orchids*
7 sprigs of lily-of-the-valley	*2 porcelaine rosebuds*	*3 porcelaine rosebuds*	*5 sprigs of lily-of-the-valley*
7 porcelaine rosebuds (all-in-one roses)	*1 porcelaine half rose*	*3 porcelaine half-roses*	*5 porcelaine rosebuds*
5 porcelaine half-roses		*1 full porcelaine rose*	*5 porcelaine half-roses*
1 porcelaine full rose			*1 full porcelaine rose*

Paste
Pale melon, pale green, mid green

•

Cutters
freesia (575, 574)

•

Wire
24-gauge white and green

•

Tape
White

•

Dusts
Choose colours to tone with the flowers on the cake, primrose yellow, apple green

FREESIA

 Use only the stalks from the stamens, having removed the heads. Dip them into egg white, then into the dust you will use to colour the flower. Dip the moistened stamen tips into this, back in egg white, back into dust. Set aside to dry.

For the pistil, take a 24-gauge white wire. Cut a piece of white tape into four along its length. Attach a $\frac{1}{4}$ piece of tape to the wire with 24-gauge white 1 cm ($\frac{1}{2}$ inch) of tape proud of the end of the wire. Cut this into three and twiddle the tape. Position the three stamens just below the pistil.

Make a tube of pale melon paste about 3.5 cm ($1\frac{1}{2}$ inch) long. Flatten the broad end. Place the cutter over the tube and cut out the flower. Broaden every second petal a bit more than the others. Use a celstick to elongate each petal slightly. Cut small wedges of paste from between the petals of the flower. Soften the edges of the petals. Gently hook the tip of the broad petals inwards. Open the throat of the freesia with an anger tool. Make sure the slightly broader petals of the freesia are situated above the narrower petals. Paint a little primrose yellow dust into the throat of the flower, and a very small amount at the base of one of the narrower petals.

Moisten the wire holding the stamens and pistil and pull down through the tube of the flower. Make sure these pieces are below the top edge of the petals. Dust a little primrose yellow just above where the petal is fastened to the wire. Add a little apple green just below this.

To make the calyx, roll out a small piece of light/mid green paste and cut it to a diamond shape. Pull the wire through the centre of the diamond, moisten the wire and pinch the calyx into place.

Dust the edges of the petals with the colour chosen. I find it is best to dust the inside edge of the petals before dusting the outer edge. Mark a central dark line of colour very carefully down the centre of each petal.

Make some smaller half-open flowers as well.

BUD

♣ Roll a small cone of mid green paste. Insert a moistened 24-gauge green hooked wire into this. Mark three lines on the bud using a three-wire cage. Pinch the top of the bud to a point. Make more buds, each larger than the last. They get paler as they increase in size, so use pale green then pale melon paste as they get larger. Attach a calyx, as for the flower, to each of the buds.

♣ To make an opening bud, make a small cone of pale melon paste and insert a moistened 24-gauge white wire into it. Cut out a shape with the cutter. Gently soften the edges of the petals with a dog bone tool on a foam pad and cup each petal.

Attach the petals to the cone one after the other. Make sure the tube is slender and fastened securely to the wire. Dust the base of the tube as for the flower. Add a calyx as for the flower.

♣ Freesia spikes usually consist of about five to seven small buds, an opening bud, a small half-open flower and about two fully opened flowers. Assemble the flower spike by starting with a small bud. The buds and flowers should be wired together very closely and bent into place. They tend to be mounted alternately along the spike. The arm of the spike is also gently curved until after the last flower has been fastened in place. The stalks then bend sharply down.

ALL-IN-ONE ROSE

PORCELAINE ROSE

This is a very pale ivory with a pale yellow overtone. The centre is pinky apricot.

Make as for All-in-One Rose. The base colour is very pale melon. Inside the petals where they join the stem they have a soft flush of primrose yellow lightened with white petal dust. To this is added a small touch of vine green. For the colour in the centre of the rose use an equal proportion of apricot and pink, brushed on neat, but with a very light touch. The calyx is a pale to mid green.

❧ Make the rose knob using the paste in the colour chosen for the rose. The knob should fit inside one of the petals. It should have a broad base and a narrow point.

❧ *Layer 1*: Take a ball of paste in the colour you have chosen. As backing colour, take a ball of pale melon paste, half the size of the other ball. Flatten the small ball slightly and place it behind the other one. Roll out the paste with the chosen colour.

❧ Cut out a shape, using the blossom cutter. Lift the shape, then turn it over, placing it right side up on a foam pad. If you are using a metal cutter, use a fine pair of scissors to cut down further between the petals. Soften the edges of all the petals. Moisten the centre of the rose and also the whole of one petal. Lift the shape, pull a 20-gauge wire through the centre and settle the knob against the moistened petal, allowing at least 5 mm ($\frac{1}{4}$ inch) above the knob. Roll the petal tightly around the knob, making sure it cannot be seen. Call that petal No. 1.

❧ Holding the wire, leave the petal next to petal No. 1 alone and moisten the sides of the next petal, No. 3. Then leave the next and moisten the sides of petal No. 5. Pick up petal No. 3, making sure it is slightly taller than the petal surrounding the knob (No. 1), and attach one side to the knob – the join from petal No. 1 should be aimed at the middle of this petal. Then pick up petal No. 5 and stick that against the knob as well. Spiral the two petals around the centre, pulling down gently as you do so. This tightens the centre of the rose. Make sure that

these two petals do not drop below the height of petal No. 1.

❧ Repeat the above process with the two remaining petals, No. 2 and No. 4. You will have to turn the knob slightly to get the joins from petals No. 3 and No. 5 to aim at the middle of petals No. 2 and No. 4. Moisten the edges of the petals and spiral them into one another. Gently roll back the upper side edge of the two petals. If you add a calyx (see page 45) at this stage, you have a bud.

❧ *Layer 2*: Roll out the paste as before and cut out a shape with the blossom cutter. Turn the shape over on to a foam pad and soften the edges of the petals. Cup the petals. Moisten the centre of the shape. Pick up the knob with Layer 1 in place. Pull the wire through the centre of the shape, lining up the joins from layer 1 to the middle of two opposite petals. Moisten the edges of these two petals. Spiral these two petals into one another. Make sure these petals are fractionally higher than the previous layer. Roll back their upper and side edges slightly.

❧ Rotate the wire so you can moisten one of the two petals hanging down on one side of the knob. Stick this petal in place across a join. Turn the wire and moisten the edges of the petal on the opposite side from the one you have just stuck in place. Stick this petal across a join. Rotate the wire again and fasten the last petal of this layer in place. Now check to see that the last three petals are evenly spaced around the knob and are spiralled into one another. Roll back the upper side edges of these petals. At one side, roll back

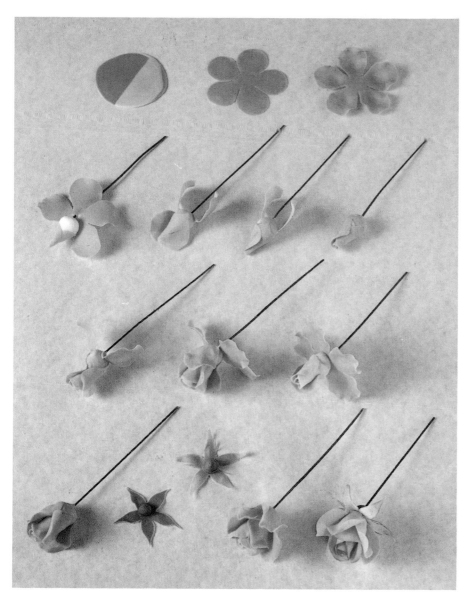

two petals so the knob is almost exposed down to the base. If you add a calyx (see Tip box) at this stage, you have a half-rose.

* *Layer 3*: Roll out the paste as before, soften the edges and cup the petals, making the cupping a bit stronger than for the previous layer. Using both a veiner and dresden tool, mark a line down the centre of each petal.

* The first petal in this layer to be placed in position should be covering the join where the two petals roll back a long way. Continue sticking the petals in place, one after another, always across a join. Keep going from one side to the other, so that this layer is not neatly spiralled. With a cocktail stick, roll back the upper edges and petal sides.

* Moisten the centre of the calyx, see Tip box, and stick it in place making sure the sepals are fitted across the joins of the petals. Take a cocktail stick and roll it around the calyx just below the knob. This will make an indentation just before the tube. Work the tube between your fingers getting a good join. Cut off any excess paste. Dry, then dust with chosen colour.

QUICK
LILY-OF-THE-VALLEY

Paste
White

•

Cutters
Smallest blossom plunger

•

Wire
*32- or 33-gauge white,
24-gauge*

•

Tape
Nile green

•

Dusts
*Apple green, vine green,
white*

♣ Cut 32 or 33-gauge wires into 3.5 cm (1½ inch) lengths. With a pair of tweezers or pliers make very small hooks on the wires.

♣ Each stem of lily-of-the-valley has approximately fifteen buds and flowers on it. To create the effect, make eight graduated buds and seven flowers. Make little balls of white paste for the buds, moisten the hooked wires and insert them into the balls, making sure they are still round.

♣ For the flowers, make seven slightly larger balls of white paste. Roll out another piece of white paste very thinly indeed. Holding a ball of the rolled-out paste in your left hand, cut a tiny blossom shape from the rolled-out paste with your right hand, depressing the plunger cutter on to the ball of paste and so fastening the blossom to the ball. Using a small ball tool, cup the flower. Pull a hooked, moistened wire through the flower.

♣ Tape the buds and flowers on to a 24-gauge wire. Dust the buds a pale green. With a pair of tweezers curve each little stem and the whole stalk.

JAVA ORCHID

Paste
White

•

Cutter
Stephanotis (566)

•

Wire
28-gauge white

•

Dusts
*Moss green, pink,
apricot, white, primrose*

•

Paste colour
Nasturtium

The bud is long and slender, having a fairly sharp point. Mark the bud with a five cage, and dust with pink, white and apricot mix. Dust the junction of the bud and the wire moss green.

♣ Roll a medium ball of paste into a teardrop. Insert a moistened wire into the narrow end, pushing until it almost protrudes through the rounded end. Roll the narrow end between your fingers forming a very slender tube on the wire. Flatten the broad end so it is the same shape as a rose petal. Frill the edge with a dresden tool. Press the tip firmly into the centre of the petal so the lip curves downwards and you make an indentation. Pinch the petal gently from the back, closing the indentation slightly. See that the curve at the front of the lip is pleasing. Set aside.

♣ Roll out a piece of paste fairly thinly, but leave a thicker piece at the centre (use a small hole on Mexican hat board, for the back of the shape), cut out a shape using the stephanotis cutter. Soften the edges of each petal gently. Place the flat side of the shape against a pad of foam. Using a dog bone tool, gently stroke the arms and legs from the tips inwards, cupping them and curving them gently backwards. Turn the petal over, stroke the head from the tip to the centre, cupping it gently and curving it forward. Stroke the veining tool from the tip inwards leaving a central vein down the head. Give the shape a belly button, moisten this very slightly, and pull the lip petal through, the open throat pointing upwards at the head. Pinch the back shape firmly on to the tube to attach it.

♣ Mix a little white and primrose dust and lightly dust the indentation at the centre of the lip. Mix the pink, white and apricot dust together and apply to both the rear petals, the edge of the lip and the outside of this petal.

♣ Using a very fine brush and the paste colour lightly moistened, paint a few fine lines on the lip petal and light spots of colour towards the centre of the head and arm petals. Brush a little moss green dust on to the junction of the back petal and the wire, and down the wire for the stem.

African
WEDDING CAKE

15 cm (6 inch) 23 cm
(9 inch) and 30 cm (12
inch) round cakes
23 cm (9 inch) thin round
hardboard board 40 cm
(16 inch) and 20 cm
(8 inch) round cake
boards
Champagne sugarpaste
White royal icing
3 × 23 cm (9 inch) crystal
Wilton pillars
5 Wilton flower picks

•

FOR THE SPRAYS
2 rosy cheeked lovebirds
1 large spray of
impala lilies
2 smaller sprays of
impala lilies
15 sprays of devil's root,
5 without berries,
10 with berries
5 sprays of agapanthus
10 sprays of erica
versicolor
3 sprays of freesias
7 sprays of bridal
gladiolus (painted lady)
15 sprays of shepherd's
delight
15 sprays of round
eucalyptus leaves
3 long sprays of slender
eucalyptus leaves

The birds, flowers and greenery on this cake are all indigenous to Southern Africa, the place of origin of many well-known plant species now common throughout the world.

♣ Cover the cakes and boards with champagne sugarpaste.

♣ When the sugarpaste has set, attach the 30 cm (12 inch) cake to the 40 cm (16 inch) board. The 23 cm (9 inch) cake goes on the 23 cm (9 inch) board, and the 15 cm (6 inch) cake is attached to the 20 cm (8 inch) board.

♣ Insert three crystal pillars into the 23 cm (9 inch) cake. Stack the 23 cm (9 inch) cake immediately on top of the 30 cm (12 inch) cake and fasten it in place with a fine snailtrail around the base. Pipe a snailtrail around the bases of the 15 cm (6 inch) and 30 cm (12 inch) cakes. Attach cream picot-edged ribbon around the edges of the large and small cake boards.

♣ Insert two Wilton flower picks into the front of the 30 cm (12 inch) cake. The first one is to the right of the mid line, about 2.5 cm (1 inch) from the board. The second flower pick is carefully inserted on the same level as the first, but about 4 cm (1½ inch) to the right. Make holes in the cake before inserting the flower picks.

♣ Repeat the process with the 23 cm (9 inch) tier, but here the first pick should be inserted with care above the point between the two picks on the lower tier; the second of these picks will be inserted to the right of the second pick on

the bottom tier. Keep the tips of the flower picks well away from the inserted crystal pillars.

♣ Insert a single flower pick into the back of the top tier about half way down the cake. For safety, leave the edges of the flower picks protruding slightly. Wire up the largest of the impala lily sprays using ½-width brown tape. About half-way across the top of the top tier, wire in the two lovebirds. The wires for their legs are bent outwards and bound in along the length of the stem of the impala lily spray. Add some small paste feet to the birds at this stage. Continue wiring up the spray, making it long enough to curve over the rear of the cake and bend to fit into the flower pick. Bind some of the devil's root leaf sprays on to the impala lily to add a little greenery, binding these stems on to the impala lily spray.

♣ Tape the other greenery and flowers into four sprays, mixing the colours attractively. Push the ends of these sprays into the flower picks, filling in any gaps with small clusters of flowers.

♣ Use the devil's root and sprays of slender eucalyptus leaves as the long trails for the sprays. Extended trails of devil's root should link the two lower tiers to the flowers and greenery arranged on the top tier.

AGAPANTHUS

Paste
Pale melon

•

Cutter
Agapanthus (575)

•

Stamens
Medium

•

Wire
28-gauge white,
26-gauge white,
24-gauge white

•

Dusts
Nutkin brown, jade,
cornflower blue, plum,
apple green, vine green

I have used fifteen buds and seven flowers in the clusters I have put together for the cake. The stems of the flowers and buds curve gracefully to join the central stem. They are approximately the same height, so the flowers and buds at the outer edges of the clusters have longer stems than those near the centre. The flowers are arranged slightly higher than the buds.

♣ Take three stamens and fold them in half so the heads are approximately level. An extra stamen, half the length of the three flower stamens, forms the pistil. Dust the stamen heads a dark greeny grey, using a mixture of nutkin brown and jade dust. The stamens are a pale blue changing to pale green at the base. The pistil is very short and a creamy blue. Bind the stamens and pistil to a 24-gauge white wire, remembering to position the pistil below the stamens. With a pair of tweezers, curve the stamens. The pistil remains straight.

♣ Make a tube of paste about 2.5 cm (1 inch) long. Flatten the broad end and roll it out finely. The tube should be slender enough to pass through the centre of the cutter. If it is too thick, then put the tube down the hole in a celpad and cut it in reverse. Cut out a shape. Each alternate petal is broader than the ones next to it. The cutter reflects this, but each broad petal should be broadened a bit more using a celstick or cocktail stick. Leave a thicker band of paste down the centre line of these broad petals. Lengthen each petal slightly. If the petals become distorted trim the edge with a pair of fine scissors. Soften the edges of the petals with the small end of a dog bone tool.

♣ With a veiner tool, mark a strong line down the centre of each petal on the upper side. Open the centre of the flower with a large celstick or anger tool. Moisten the base of the stamens and pull them down into the centre of the flower. Arrange the

petals attractively. The broad petals are often slightly higher than the narrower petals.

♣ Dust the petals from the outer edge with a mixture of plum and cornflower blue. The brushing must be very delicate, as the petals are pale towards the centre. Once you have dusted the outer edge of the petals, paint a strong line of colour into the vein in the middle of each petal. To control where the colour is going, it is best to moisten the dust. Dust the back of the petals cornflower blue down over the tube. Do not dust all the way to the base, as the flower fades from the blue through cream to a light green (a mixture of apple green and vine green) at the base where the paste joins the wire.

BUD

♣ Take a medium-sized piece of paste, roll it into a barrel shape and then bring one end to a slight tip. Insert a moistened, hooked wire into the broad end.

♣ Make a cage of six 28-gauge wires. Spread the wires so they are in three pairs. Insert the bud into the cage and, allowing small gaps between the pairs of wires, bite into the bud, taking the lines right down to the wire. This marking gives you the different sizes of the petals. Dust the tip of the flower with the same colour used for dusting the petals.

♣ The flowers and buds may be used in arrangements as though they have been 'pipped' by a florist, or they can be used in their growing clusters. Some flower heads have a great many buds and flowers wired together.

Rosy cheeked lovebirds

❧ Roll a ball of paste into a barrel shape, to form the head and body. Pinch to a point at the front of the head, then use scissors to cut the beak in two. Use a dresden tool to curve the upper beak. Make the nostrils using a scriber and holes for the eyes. Roll pieces of black paste into balls and fill the eye sockets.

❧ Feather the bodies using a bark tool and scriber. Using the wing moulds, make the tails and wings, curving them with a dog bone tool and dresden tool. Frill the upper edge of the wings and the bottom edge of the tail.

❧ Insert a hairpin shaped piece of wire through the lower body for the legs. Attach wings and tail. Leave the beak white. Mark a white ring around the eye.

❧ Dust the top of the head with red and pink. Under the throat and cheeks, dust with the pink and apricot mixed. Lightly dust the back of the head and the underside of the bird with primrose yellow tinted with vine green. Add a little more vine green. Dust both sides of the wings. The upper back is dark blue, lighter towards the tail.

❧ Bend the wire sideways and tape the birds on the impala lily. Add white highlight to the eye.

EUCALYPTUS LEAVES

✿ Eucalyptus may produce up to three different shaped leaves on a twig. Round leaves are new growth, oval leaves are semi-mature leaves and strap-like leaves are fully mature. You may choose to use just one shape. Small eucalyptus trees have been hybridized to produce leaves in all three forms. The leaves can also be opposite or alternate. Round-leafed varieties are usually arranged as opposites. Their stalks are so short as to be almost non-existent, and the pairs of leaves are very close together. This variety has a lot more leaves per stem than the oval or strap-shaped leaves. Another leaf can be made with the side petal of a slipper orchid, which is like a figure of eight.

✿ Roll out light grey-green paste thinly on a grooved board. Cut out leaf shapes, insert a short, moistened 28-gauge white wire into the central vein of each leaf. Soften the edges without frilling the leaves. It is noticeable that the veining on some of the more round leaves can also ray out! Using a veining tool make a strong central vein down the centre of each leaf. If you use the circle cutters (for round leaves) you can soften the shape slightly by rolling out the tip of the leaf to form a slight point.

✿ Dust the leaves very delicately with a little grey dust, then white dust on its own and finally the back and margins with a warm burgundy colour (made by mixing plum, red and nutkin brown together). Some varieties are very silvery in colour; use silver lustre or mother-of-pearl highlighter. Glaze with a $\frac{1}{2}$-glaze.

✿ Tape individual leaves on to a heavy wire such as 22-gauge which allows you to arrange the foliage where you want it.

SILVER TREE
(*Leucadendron Argenteum*)

✿ Roll out the pale green paste leaving a thickened central vein. Cut out a number of each size of leaf. Insert a moistened wire into each leaf ensuring the wire is inserted almost to the tip of the leaf. Soften the edges of the leaves then vein them. Gently shape and curve the leaves pinching the tips of the leaves slightly together. Dust the leaves very lightly with some of the green petal dust, the tips with rose and red petal dust and then top with a strong dusting of the silver lustre colour. This will make it more subtle.

✿ Make a small cone of the green paste, insert a hooked 26-gauge wire into the cone. Snip the cone into spikes with scissors. Dust with the green and silver lustre colour.

✿ Using $\frac{1}{2}$ width white tape fasten the cone and leaves to a 22-gauge $\frac{1}{2}$ length wire. Closely surround and cup the cone with about three layers of the leaves in varying sizes. The remaining leaves are spiralled down the stem getting smaller and sparser. Dust the stem with a mixture of the red and rose dust.

DEVIL'S ROOT

Paste
Mid green, ruby red

•

Cutters
(LC3) Speckled abutilon

•

Veiner
Jellima

•

Stamens
Black miniature stamen off-cuts

•

Wire
*28-gauge white,
22-gauge, 18-gauge*

•

Tape
Nile green

•

Dusts
*Dark green mixture,
moss green, red*

♣ Roll out the mid green paste using a grooved rolling pin or grooved board. Cut out the leaf shapes using the above cutters, using all three sizes. Use fewer small leaves than the medium and large.

♣ Insert ¼-length, moistened white 28-gauge wires into the central veins of the leaves. Using ¼-width tape, cover the white wires.

♣ Vein the leaves with the jellima veiner and, using a dresden tool, serrate the edge of the leaves. Pinch the leaf towards the central vein and set aside to firm up. Dust the leaves down the centre with a dash of the dark green mixture, go over this lightly with a coating of moss green dust. Glaze with a ½-glaze.

♣ Make the berries by inserting short, hooked wires into small balls of ruby red paste. Insert a piece of off-cut stamen into each berry, leaving it protruding slightly. Dust the berries with red petal dust and glaze with a full glaze.

♣ Start the tip of the trail of leaves with a piece of ½-width tape protruding about 5 cm (2 inch) from the front of the wire. Twiddle this to a fine strand and twirl it artistically. Tape the leaves on to the central wire alternately. The stems of the leaves should be left long – about 2.5 cm (1 inch) long for the small leaves increasing to about 3 cm (1½ inch) long for the larger leaves. The leaves should also be taped on to the wire about 2.5 cm (1 inch) apart for the small leaves, also increasing to a gap of about 3 cm (1½ inch) for the larger leaves. About every third leaf should also have a tendril emerging from the leaf axil. These should be between 5–7.5 cm (2–3 inch) long, the longer tendrils emerging from the leaf axil of the larger leaves.

♣ To make these tendrils, bind a piece of ¼-tape on to the end of a ¼-length 28-gauge wire, leaving about 2.5 cm (1 inch) of tape protruding from the end. Twiddle this to form a fine strand. Bind the tendril loosely around a celstick to curve it gently. Tape them in with the leaves as described above.

♣ The berries should be bound into clusters of three to five and bound on to the stem of the leaf trails alternately, at the junction of a leaf to the stem.

ERICA *(Erica Versicolor)*

Paste
Pale melon, mid green

•

Cutters
*Small calyx cutter (406)
(With a fine-nosed pair of
pliers, gently pinch each
sepal slightly together on
one side. This gives you
two sizes of cutter in one.
On this occasion use the
smaller cutter), tiny
blossom cutter*

•

Dusts
*Egg yellow, primrose
yellow, rose, red, moss
green*

•

Wire
*30-gauge white,
24-gauge white*

•

Stamens
Tiny stamens

•

Tape
Mid green

♣ Roll a tiny ball of pale melon paste into a fine tube. Flatten the end and roll out finely. Cut out using the smaller edge of the small calyx cutter. Gently hollow the tube about half way up, flaring the lip slightly at the end. Gently soften the lip with your fingers. Fasten a single stamen to the wire, dust the head with the moss green and the thread with lightened egg yellow, with a fine dust of red on one side. Dust the lip of the flower with lightened egg yellow and then very delicately with a dusting of moss green.

♣ Thread the moistened wire of the stamen through the flower and position it so the stamen protrudes from the front of the flower. Round the end of the tube and dust it with a mixture of rose and red dust. Roll out a piece of mid green paste and, using a tiny blossom cutter, cut out a small green calyx. Fasten this on to the moistened tube of the flower. Wire the flowers and buds into clusters of three. The tips of the buds are a noticeably dark green.

♣ Add fine thread-like leaves to the branches holding the sprays of flowers. To do this slash full-width mid green tape into fine strips. Bind around the wires and the fine leaves will spiral around the wire. Fasten them all on to a long firm stem which is also decorated with the cut tape leaves, lower down, as the leaves become heavier, this can be emulated by twisting the tape into fine threads. The flowers and buds are all arranged on one side of the stem, and the stem curves towards that same side, rather like assembling lily-of-the-valley (see page 46).

Erica buds The buds are small, elongated pieces of paste, gently indented using a five-wire cage.

IMPALA LILY

♣ Tape a ½-width piece of white tape on to a 24-gauge white wire, leaving about 1 cm (½ inch) above the wire. With a fine pair of scissors, cut this tape into five lengthwise. Dust the edges of the tape with a delicate flush of rose and red dust mixed together. Gently twist these pieces of tape into a loose spiral. Attach five small white stamens just below the spiralled tape.

♣ Roll a medium piece of white paste into a ball. Make a long medium-sized tube. Cut out a shape with the larger calyx cutter. Open the throat with a celstick. With the celstick in the throat of the flower, press the tube against the orchid veiner to get some strong straight veins on the outside of the tube below each petal.

♣ Roll out another piece of white paste flat. Cut out another shape with the smaller calyx cutter. Cut a V-shape into the point of the calyx. Cut small slashes into the shape on either side of the V. Roll it out again, softening the cut pieces, but keeping the shape. If you lose the V-shapes, cut them out again. Insert this piece into the throat of the flower made with the larger calyx cutter. Make sure the V-shaped indentations are positioned at the junction of the outer petals, slightly higher than the petals, forming a coronet.

♣ Using a five-pointed pineapple tool, mark the centre of each of the outer petals. Turning the flower gently, mark two shorter, lighter lines on either side of the central vein. Using a dresden tool, frill the edge of the outer petals. Go over this frilling again with a blunt cocktail stick. Using a veining tool, mark a central vein down the centre of each petal, starting it in the vein marked into the throat of the flower but behind the coronet. Pinch the tip of each petal to a sharp point.

♣ Very carefully dust the frilled edges of the petal with a mixture of rose and red petal dust. Mix some of this dust with a little liquid and carefully paint three lines inside the throat below each petal. Do not get any of the colour on to the coronet.

♣ Moisten the wire on the stamens with a little egg white, pull the stamens and pistil into the throat of the flower, leaving them protruding slightly. Paint lines of rose red colour on to the outside of the tube using the lines pressed into the tube as guidelines. Fasten a few small bracts of the greeny brown paste around the base of the flower.

Bud: Make small slender cones of white paste on the wires. Allow to dry. Cut out the shapes with the larger cutter and, using a dresden tool, frill the edge of the outer petals. Dust the edges of the petals with a mixture of rose and red and then very carefully stick the petals into place around the small cone. The petals must be spiralled. Use the orchid veiner to mark the tube as for the flower. Paint on lines of rose-red colour.

♣ Some very small buds can be simply made using a five-wired cage. Pinch the paste between your fingers firmly, spiral the petals, and then very carefully dust them with the mixture of rose and red colour, before tightening the buds. Mark the tubes and colour as before.

♣ The same greeny brown bracts are arranged at the base of the buds as for the flowers.

Paste
White, pale greeny brown

•

Cutters
Rose calyces (248 and 304)

•

Veiner
Orchid

•

Stamens
Small white

•

Wire
24-gauge white

•

Tape
White

•

Dusts
Rose, red

SHEPHERD'S DELIGHT

Paste
White, mid green

•

Cutters
*Small blossom (F10),
smallest calyx (R15)*

•

Stamens
*Five miniature yellow
stamens*

•

Wire
28-gauge white

•

Tape
Nile green

•

Dusts
*Plum, fuchsia, lemon
yellow*

•

Paste colour
Ruby

♣ Using a ¼-piece of tape, fasten five short stamens on to a 28-gauge white wire. Dip them in a little lemon yellow dust.

♣ Roll out a piece of white paste on a Mexican hat board using a small back and cut out the flower using the small blossom cutter. Place the flower face down on a non-stick board and, using the medium celstick, elongate each petal slightly so they become oval-shaped.

♣ Soften the edge of the petals with a dog bone tool, resting the petal on a foam pad. Lightly mark a central vein down the centre of each petal using a dresden tool. Turn the flower over and open the throat with a celstick.

♣ Moisten the base of the stamens slightly and insert the wire holding the stamens through the centre of the flower.

♣ Paint a fine line of ruby paste colour into the central line marked with the veining tool. Add a little more in small

triangles of colour for the inside of the calyx showing between the petals. Dust the outside of the petals with plum dust mixed with a greater quantity of fuchsia pink.

♣ Roll out a small piece of mid green paste. Cut out a small shape using the calyx cutter and stick this over the back of the flower, positioning the calyces between the petals. Dust very lightly with a little plum and fuchsia colour mixture.

♣ To make a bud, take a small piece of white paste, roll it into an oval, insert a moistened, hooked 28-gauge wire into one end. Mark on five petals using a five-cage, dust lightly with plum and fuchsia. Add a small green calyx from mid green paste moistened with a little egg white. Lightly dust the green calyx with plum/fuchsia mixture.

♣ Wire the flowers and buds into clusters of between three to five.

BRIDAL GLADIOLUS

Paste
White, mid green

•

Cutters
Bridal gladiolus (597 and 598)

•

Veiners
Corn-on-the-cob or poppy petal veiner

•

Stamens
Medium lily

♣ Tape a ¼-width piece of white tape over a 26-gauge white wire, leaving 1 cm (½ inch) tape above the wire. Using scissors, cut this into three and twiddle each piece into a fine strand. Cut off a little of the excess tape and bend the pieces backwards, evenly spaced.

♣ Take three stamens. Colour their two ridges with a fine layer of black. Dust the stamens and threads with lightened primrose.

♣ Using a grooved board or rolling pin, roll out three large

petals. Insert moistened 30-gauge white wire into the central veins. Vein them with a corn-on-the-cob or poppy veiner. Using a cocktail stick, soften the edges of two of the three petals, frilling gently. Using a dresden tool, mark a broad shallow V-vein down the centre. The tip of these petals should be pinched in gently while placed on foam. They curve backwards from the central vein.

♣ The third or central petal should be softened and frilled

Wire
30-gauge white, 26-gauge white

•

Tape
White

•

Dusts
Primrose yellow, plum, red, black, mulberry

Dust the lower centre of each small petal with lightened yellow. Large petals are white with a pale yellow base, with plum/red nectar guidelines. The three small petals have a flame-shaped white centre and plum/red flash.

more strongly than the two side petals. Using a large ball tool, cup the middle of this petal, forcing it to curve gently. Reinforce the centre vein with a veining tool.

❧ Cut out three small petals and wire as for the larger petals. Vein them with the corn-on-the-cob or poppy veiner. Soften the edge of the petals with a cocktail stick. Using the dresden tool, vein two of the petals on the underside, curving them gently backwards over this veining. The third or middle petal should be veined strongly down the centre using the veining tool and the front edges of this petal should be rolled back gently from the tip. Gently pinch this petal to a soft point. Set it aside to dry in a gentle curve, following the same lines as the two small side petals.

❧ To assemble the flower, position the pistil behind the stamens. The large central petal curves forward over these pieces. The two large side petals go behind and to the side of the large central petal, curving backwards. The two small side petals go below and to the side of the small middle petal, which is immediately below the stamens. The flower's back is protected by two long curved bracts, made from mid green paste.

❧ The buds are petal tips protruding from two bracts. The leaves are long parallel-veined strap leaves. The bracts are mid green paste cut into long, narrow strips with gently pointed ends. Run a veining tool down the centre. Moisten the lower edge and fasten, cupping the flower.

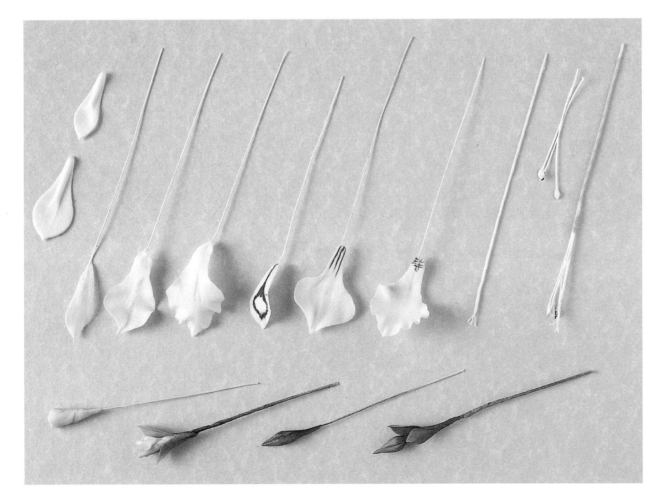

Christmas Rose Cake

The pale, open faces of the Christmas roses contrast superbly with the dark sprays of ivy leaves on this impressive cake, made to look like an arrangement in a vase.

1 rich fruit cake baked in a 1.2 litre (2 pint) ovenproof glass bowl
30 cm (12 inch) scalloped cake board
Mid green sugarpaste
Celpot
5 small celpicks
Equal quantities of mid green, pink and champagne sugarpaste rolled together and marbled

•

FOR THE SPRAY
25 sprays of large ivy leaves; 5 long, 12 medium and 8 short (see page 16)
5 sprays of dark birdsfoot ivy (see page 17)
15 Christmas roses
3 half-open Christmas rosebuds
5 Christmas rosebuds

❀ Completely surround the cake in marzipan. Starting with the top, cover with green sugarpaste and allow to set. Coat the domed side with the marbled paste. It is important that the marbled paste is visible all around the edge of the top of the cake, as this makes the edge of the vase. Set aside to dry.

❀ At the same time, make the base by filling an appropriate-sized saucer with the marbled sugarpaste (after dusting the curved side of the sugarpaste with icing sugar). Press it in firmly, then turn it out. Immediately after turning it out, indent the top of the saucer-shaped piece of moulded sugarpaste with the base of the bowl in which the cake was baked. Set this aside to dry.

❀ Insert the celpot into the cake following the instructions on the packaging, and add five small celpicks around the edge to take the extra flowers. This has to be done very carefully, taking out small piece of cake with a very sharp, thin bladed knife. If the cake is left in place the outer edge might split. If the celpicks are left out all the flowers would have to come from the centre of the cake, thus spoiling the effect.

❀ Arrange the buds, flowers and leaf sprays in the celpot and celpicks. Some pieces obviously have to be wired together to fasten them into the picks, but gently prise them apart so they look as though they are arranged in a vase.

❀ Cover the board with a piece of velvet; this is most easily done either using tacky glue or spray glue. The thick tacky glue will not mark the velvet, but use the spray glue sparingly as this can soak through the fabric. Cut off the excess cloth, and stick the loose edges under the board very neatly but firmly.

❀ Stick the saucer-shaped piece of paste on to the board and allow it to dry. Attach the cake itself (with flowers in place) to this shape using royal icing. Support the cake in this position until the royal icing is very dry. If you move the cake too soon the whole arrangement might become unstable.

CHRISTMAS ROSE

Paste
*White, mid green, light
green*

•

Cutters
*Christmas rose (282 and
283), miniature daisy
(107), simple leaf (231)*

•

Veiner
Curved Christmas rose

•

Stamens
*Medium hammerseed
white stamens*

•

Wire
*24-gauge white,
28-gauge white, a little
fine florist's wire,
22-gauge uncovered*

•

Tape
Nile green

•

Dusts
*Dark green mixture, vine
green, fuchsia, plum,
white, primrose yellow,
lemon yellow, moss green*

♣ Take a piece of full width green tape. Make four cuts, about 1 cm ($\frac{1}{2}$ inch) long into the width of the tape, dividing it into five threads. Below the cuts, bind the tape on to $\frac{1}{3}$ length of 24-gauge wire. Twiddle each of the cut threads into a finer thread, curve them outwards from the centre and cut the tips off neatly.

♣ Fold about twenty-five medium hammerseed stamens in half and bind them loosely together using a piece of fine florist's wire. Dip them into a mixture of the lemon and primrose yellow, then dust off the excess dust. Insert the wire holding the pistil through the centre of the loosely wired stamens, leave the pistil slightly proud of the stamens, and bind the florist's wire tightly around the central stem. Tape over the lower edge of the stamens with a piece of $\frac{1}{4}$-width tape.

♣ To make the flower, roll out a piece of pale green paste quite finely and cut out a shape with the miniature daisy cutter. Elongate the petals a little; use a blunt cocktail stick and broaden each petal slightly, leaving them slightly cupped. Moisten the centre of this shape slightly and fasten this on to the central stem immediately behind the stamens.

♣ To make the tepals, roll out a piece of white paste fairly thinly, using the grooved rolling pin or grooved board. Cut out five tepals, insert a moistened $\frac{1}{3}$-length white 28-gauge wire into each tepal, pushing it in as far as it will go. Use the blunt cocktail stick to flute the edge of each tepal slightly (if you flute it too heavily once you vein it it will squash the edges into pleats).

♣ Vein each tepal with the Christmas rose veiner. Reinforce the fluting with the blunt cocktail stick without removing too much veining. Pinch the tip of each tepal together slightly. Set the tepals aside to dry for a few minutes.

♣ Dust the inside of each tepal from the centre out with a mixture of the lemon, primrose and white petal dusts, adding a quick dash of the vine green on top. The outside of the tepals should be dusted with a mixture of the fuchsia, plum and white in a slashing motion from the centre out to create lines of colour.

♣ To make the bracts, roll out a piece of the mid green paste using a grooved rolling pin or grooved board. Cut out two shapes with the simple leaf cutter. Soften the edges with a blunt cocktail stick or a dog bone tool, insert a moistened 28-gauge wire into each and set aside to firm up slightly. Dust with some of the dark green mixture from the centre, then go over the whole bract with a thin coating of moss green dust. Catch a little of the fuchsia and plum mixture from the tepals along the edges of the bracts. Dip into a $\frac{1}{2}$-glaze.

♣ Tape the tepals behind the flower, using the green shape. The first two tepals to be bound in place are positioned between two and three o'clock and nine and ten o'clock.

♣ Behind these bind in a tepal at twelve o'clock and two others between four and five o'clock and seven and eight o'clock. Bind in a 22-gauge wire to add strength to the stems.

♣ Using ½-width tape, tape several layers over the main stem.

♣ About 1 cm (½ inch) behind the tepals, bind in the two bracts, alongside one another.

Bud: Take a large piece of white paste and shape into a teardrop. Cover a hooked 22-gauge wire with green tape and insert it into the paste. Make a five-wire cage, insert the point of the bud into the cage. Gather the wires up evenly along the stem, pull the cage in opposite directions so the wires bite into the paste. While the cage is still in place, gently pinch the paste protruding between the wires into fine 'petals'. Remove the cage and spiral these 'petals' attractively around one another. Thicken the stem with tape. Using a pair of pliers, gently bend the neck of the bud to an attractive angle. Tape in a pair of bracts. Dust the bud with the fuchsia and plum dust.

♣ The stems of buds, half-opened buds and flowers should all be coloured with the dark green and moss green dust on the front, and the fuchsia/plum colour down the back.

Christmas roses have very fleshy stems. The roses and buds have a slight gleam which can be created by steaming very lightly to remove the dusty look.

Patio
PERFECTION

2 × 15 cm (6 inch) round
cakes
Marzipan
Dark green sugarpaste
Champagne sugarpaste
Dark green pastillage
(see page 102)
A little darker green
sugarpaste
40 cm (16 inch) round
cake board
15 cm (6 inch) thin cake
card
18 cm (7 inch) perspex
flower holder
Celpot

•

FOR THE FLORAL
ARRANGEMENT
3 sprays of nasturtiums,
buds and leaves between
36 and 38 cm (14 and 15
inch) long
2 sprays of nasturtiums,
buds and leaves 25 and 30
cm (10 and 12 inch) long

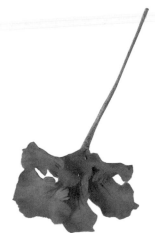

This cake was designed with a keen gardener in mind; it would be ideal to celebrate a retirement. I also wanted to use the tole work on a cake and this seemed appropriate.

♣ To make the watering can, use a tin slightly smaller than the tin used to bake the cakes to mark a curve on to the slightly rounded top of the cake. You then have a crescent shape around an ellipse. Cut the cake along this curve, about 2.5 cm (1 inch) deep. Place a few small 2.5 cm (1 inch) cubes of wood (or stock cubes) into the tin the cakes were baked in. Lower the cake back into the tin to rest on the pieces of wood, thus leaving it 2.5 cm (1 inch) above the upper lip of the cake tin. Use a long, sharp knife to cut the ellipse section of the cake away.

♣ Place the flat bottom of the cake on the thin cake card and marzipan over both the cake and the card. Make sure the base is neatly finished off as any distortion will show through.

♣ Place the domed top of the cake downwards, fill in the gap around the base with a little extra marzipan and then carefully marzipan the cake using the bandage method so you get a very flat, sharp edge to the top.

♣ Place the shaped, domed cake on its thin board directly on top of the other cake. Make sure you have a good join between the two without any gaps. Ensure the sides are all even as well.

♣ Cover the large board with champagne sugarpaste. Use one of the plastic texturing sheets to give interest to the 'patio'. Use an icing straight edge to mark the paving blocks. You can either dust or airbrush colour on to the sugarpaste to create the right effect.

♣ Sugarpaste the two cakes together using the dark green sugarpaste. It is easier to use the bandage method once again for the sides. Read the celpot instructions and insert this into the ellipse part of the top cake.

♣ The spout is formed by rolling a thick piece of sugarpaste around the perspex flower holder, making it thicker at one end. Trim the sugarpaste level at this end. Push a piece of wooden dowling into the perspex tube (it shouldn't be too tight a fit as it must be easy to remove). Leave about 6 cm (2½ inch) of the perspex tube uncovered. The sugarpaste that will fit against the cake should be cut at an angle so that a neat join will result. Moisten this end of the sugarpaste. Push the uncovered section of the perspex tube into the cake at an angle, fitting the spout snugly against the cake. Using the wooden dowling protruding from the perspex tube as a handle, support the spout until dry.

♣ Carefully remove the wooden dowling. Roll out a piece of

sugarpaste the same colour as that used for the body of the watering can and the spout. Cut it large enough to fit over the tip of the spout. Pierce neat holes into it to form the sprinkler, moisten the edges and stick in place. Neaten all the cut edges with a narrow roll of the darker green paste.

❀ Roll a piece of pastillage into a sausage, shape into a handle and set aside to dry. Once it is dry,

attach it to the watering can with a little gum glue or royal icing. Support in place until set.

❀ Very carefully position the cake on the base board.

❀ Wire up the sprays of nasturtiums until you achieve the lengths specified above.

❀ Dust the foam in the celpot to the same colour as the watering can. Carefully arrange the nasturtiums to cascade from it.

If you sugarpaste straight over the cake the edges of the watering can become indistinct. Spray the can with aerosol confectioners' glaze. Paint a decorative piece of tole work on to the side.

NASTURTIUM

Paste
Pale melon, orange, peach, red, claret, pale green

•

Cutters
Nasturtium (446–448), blossom (F9–F10) calyx (526 and 249)

•

Veiners
Nasturtium petal, nasturtium leaf

•

Stamens
Tiny yellow stamens

•

Wire
28-gauge white and green, 26-gauge green, 24-gauge green

•

Tape
Pale green

•

Dusts
Dark green mixture, moss green, apple green, lemon yellow, brown, nutkin brown, red, apricot, skintone, nasturtium

✿ Using a grooved rolling pin or board, roll out paste in the chosen colour. Cut three petals using the fringed petal cutter (446). Moisten the tips of three 28-gauge white wires and insert a wire into the central vein of each petal, taking the wire at least half-way up the broad section of the petal. Vein the petals. Roll the narrow part of each petal into a slender tube. Frill the edge of the upper section of each petal using a cocktail stick. Cut the medium section of each petal into a fringe of fine threads of paste parallel to the wire. Pinch the petals from the rear, reinforcing the central vein. Dust the petals the colour you prefer. Gently lift the fringe of each petal so that it is pointing upwards. Arrange the upper part of each petal to curve backwards. Set aside to dry.

✿ Using the grooved rolling pin or board, roll out more paste and cut out two of the second petal (447). The moistened tip of a 28-gauge white wire should be inserted into the central vein of each petal, about half-way up the broad section. Vein the petals, frill the edges firmly with a cocktail stick and pinch from the rear to reinforce the central vein. Paint varying length lines of burgundy red on the petals to form the nectar guides. Dust the petals and curve back the upper section gracefully.

✿ Fasten five tiny stamens and one slightly larger stamen, which has been dusted green, to a 26-gauge green wire. Gently curve the stamens in one direction. When the petals are firm but not brittle, wire around the stamens. Wire the two unfringed petals next to one another with stamens curving towards them. The three fringed petals are wired on either side and opposite them. Trim excess wire.

✿ Add a tiny piece of petal colour paste to the pale green paste to make a slightly yellowy green. Roll a ball of this paste into a teardrop shape. Turn the narrow end into a long, slender tube and flatten the broad end. Roll out the paste until it is fine. Cut out one of the calyx shapes, positioning the tube at the top of the single narrow sepal which is found between the two broader sepals. This is the nectary. Soften the edges of the sepals and run a veining tool from the tip to the centre of each, with the tube positioned below. Open the throat of the nectary with a small celstick. Moisten the centre of the calyx and pull the stem of the flower through it. Each sepal should be positioned between two petals, and the nectary should be between the two unfringed petals showing the nectar guides.

✿ Using pale green tape, thicken the stem slightly. Steam the flowers before wiring.

Leaves: Nasturtium leaves are peltate. Roll out a ball of pale green paste over a small hole on a Mexican hat board. With each leaf place the protrusion into the slight dip on the lower half of a nasturtium leaf veiner and vein the leaf. Cut away excess paste from the mark left by the veiner.

✿ Make round hooks on 26-gauge green wires. Bend the hooks to a 90° angle. To attach a wire to a leaf, heat the hook with a cigarette lighter and touch the

For buds, make a tiny teardrop of paste the same colour as the flower. Form into a squat, slightly pointed bud with a slender tail. Make a tiny hook at the end of a 28 gauge wire, moisten it and insert into the thick part of the bud. Mark into five with a very fine five-wire cage. Tape the wire with $\frac{1}{4}$-width pale green tape. Curve the stem wire towards the front point of the bud, and curve the tail in the same direction. (Some buds' tails can be left pointing out behind them).

Make half-open buds using a blossom cutter. Cut out a layer of petals, frill and gather them on to a 28-gauge hooked wire. Make the calyx as described for the flower, only using a smaller cutter. Attach and close around the blossom petals. Dust the petals in the same colours as the flower. The smaller the bud, the greener the calyx. As the buds develop the calyx becomes a more yellowy green. Steam the buds before wiring the plant together.

protrusion sticking up from the leaf with the red hot wire. Do not press down or you will burn through the leaf or leave a round ring on the upper surface.

♣ Dust the leaves when leather-hard. Use the dark green mixture in the centre, dust the edges with a mixture of apple green and lemon yellow, and then brush a layer of moss green over the whole leaf to blend the colours.

♣ Allow to harden and then glaze with a $\frac{1}{2}$-glaze. When dry,

use a craft knife to scrape pale veins along those left by the veiner.

♣ Start wiring the sprays of nasturtiums from the small leaves, gradually adding small buds, then larger leaves and buds until you get to the flowers, which are positioned above the leaves. Tape all leaf, bud and flower stems with the same pale green tape. The stems are a light greeny yellow colour. Dust until a natural effect is achieved. Spray carefully with aerosol confectioners' glaze.

DRIED AND PRESSED FLOWERS

This is a section of sugarcraft flowers not previously covered in a book.

The dried sugar flowers make a marvellous table decoration for an autumn festivity such as a harvest supper, and can also be used most attractively on a cake, particularly for a man. They can be tackled by anyone with well practised basic skills.

The pressed sugar flowers make unusual, delicately coloured decorations for pastillage plates, sweet boxes, place cards, wall mounted plaques or greetings cards. This is an excellent medium for beginners in sugarcraft.

2 oval cork mats, 36 cm (14 inch) and 30 cm (12 inch) fastened to one another
Piece of driftwood for backing
9 larch twigs
9 medium and small lotus pods
5 sprays of pearl grass
5 sprays of Chinese lanterns
5 poppy heads
1 spray of rose hips
3 sprays of honesty
3 sprays of beech leaves
3 sprays of oak leaves and acorns

Dried Flower
ARRANGEMENT

This was designed purely as a decorative piece. It could be used as a room decoration providing the atmosphere is kept very dry, or used alongside a cake. The driftwood could also be modelled in sugar.

♣ Start the arrangement by positioning the larch twigs in place. The Chinese lanterns and honesty should be positioned next as they are also tall elements. The poppy heads and rose hips should be added next, then the beech sprays.

♣ The oak leaves and acorn sprays should be used together with the lotus pods to hide all the mechanics of the arrangement.

Paste
Pale orange, nasturtium

•

Cutters
Large calyx cutters (244, 245) or (R11B and R11C)

•

Veiner
Clematis montana

•

Wire
20-gauge

•

Tape
White

•

Dusts
Orange, red, vine and apple green

CHINESE LANTERNS
(*Physalis*)

♣ To make the sepals take a large piece of nasturtium paste and roll into a smooth ball. Form a column which should be no longer or broader than the broad part of the sepal. The paste should be flattened out and rolled out thicker than is normal, but not so thick that the paste sticks in the cutters. Cut out the shape with the calyx cutter. Roll each of the sepals until they are just over 2.5 cm (1 inch) long. Broaden each sepal slightly, leaving a thickened ridge in the centre. The edges of the sepals should be kept even in shape or difficulties occur when you try to join them together.

♣ Using a celstick or skewer, make a shallow depression into the column from the flat side of the shape. Make a hole through the column with a wire or cocktail stick. Placing the veiner with the groove down on your board, carefully position the sepals on the veiner one at a time with a tip of the sepal lying in the groove. Make sure the sepal is straight along the groove. Position the upper veiner over the sepal and press firmly. A clear impression of the veining should be seen standing up on the side of the sepals showing the depression. Continue the veining into the centre of the depression with the cranked tweezers. Hook the tip of a 20-gauge wire with the pliers.

♣ Thicken the wire with white tape. This is better than using green tape because the stem of the Chinese lantern is orange closest to the fruit, gradually turning green as it approaches the stem. Pull the wire through the

column, leaving the hook free just above the tip of the column. Using a cigarette lighter, heat the hook until it is red hot then pull it quickly into the column. It should sizzle and smell like candyfloss as the sugar melts. The wire emerges through the hollow depression you made earlier. Fasten the sugar firmly to the wire, being careful not to get anywhere near the melted sugar or the hot wire or you could burn yourself badly. This method may seem a little hazardous, but it does give a very firm join without waiting for the sugar to dry.

♣ Pull the sepals over the column. Moisten the inner edges of the sepals with egg white and pinch firmly together, matching the tips first. If you have difficulty pinching the edges together with your fingers you may find it easier using the cranked tweezers.

♣ Dust the seedhead with a mixture of orange and red, dusting a small amount of vine and apple dust into the hollow from which the wire emerges, and also at the tip of the seedhead. Once the seedheads are dry you can glaze them with a $\frac{1}{2}$-glaze.

♣ You may like to make the top seedheads smaller than those further down the stem. These smaller seedheads are usually also a pale green colour rather than the more usual orange. For effect you might like to tone some of the seedheads from the pale green at the tips to a more orangey colour closer to the stem. There are usually between five and nine seedheads to a stem.

♣ The top of the stem is surmounted by three small green leaves. The small green seedheads have small leaves attached. For each seedhead there is a pair of leaves bracketing them. The leaves are dusted a fairly sharp green, and are glazed with a $\frac{1}{4}$-glaze.

As you work around the fruit some of the sections you have joined together may gape open. Don't let this worry you – just persevere; once you have mastered the knack it is an easy piece to make.

LOTUS SEEDHEADS

Paste
Dark brown with a touch of black

•

Wire
20-gauge, taped and thickened with dark brown tape

•

Dusts
Brown, nutkin brown, black

Lotus seedheads look very good coloured gold when used as a table decoration at Christmas, particularly if used in conjunction with gold-coloured Chinese lanterns.

♣ Take a large ball of paste and shape it into a cone. Hollow it out roughly at the upper broad end. Indent the sides of the hollow cone into many pleats and grooves. Cut the top edge level.

♣ Hook the wire, moisten it or heat it with a cigarette lighter and imbed it into the pointed end of the cone. Set it aside to dry.

♣ Once the wired cone is dry take another ball of paste, roll it into a rough, thick circle. Using a celstick or a skewer, make holes in the circle of paste, pushing the implement right through so there is a slight ridge where it emerges. The holes should be evenly spaced. On some pods they are arranged in circles, on others randomly.

♣ Dust the inside of the cone with black, then moisten with egg white. Attach the circle with holes to the top of the wired, dry cone. The circle can be flat or domed as they come in different varieties. Press it firmly on to the cone to get a good join. Cut off excess paste and neaten the edge.

♣ Dust the cone with brown, nutkin brown and a little black dust. The outer surface should be a little lighter than the very dark inside. Once the seedhead is dry, glaze it with a $\frac{3}{4}$-glaze.

PEARL GRASS
or Quaking Grass

Paste
Very pale ivory

•

Wire
32-gauge reel wire or 33-gauge straight wire, 24-gauge

•

Tape
White

•

Dusts
Champagne, white

♣ Make twenty-one very small balls of paste and roll them into tiny carrot shapes. Insert a 24-gauge hooked wire moistened with egg white into the broad end of the carrot shape. Gently flatten between your fingers. The seedheads must not be completely flat, as they are slightly rounded.

♣ With a very sharp pair of fine scissors, gently snip the edge of the seedhead from the tip moving back to the broad end. The snips should be angled backwards and should almost reach the centre line. Turn the seedhead over and repeat the snipping process, only this time remember to keep the cuts between those made before or you will cut the seedhead in half! Re-form the edges so they are joined together. Gently press the back of a modelling knife into the paste from broad to narrow ends down the centre line. Turn the seedhead over and mark in the centre line again.

♣ Dust the seedheads with champagne dust, lightened with white, gather the wired ends together and fasten on to 24-gauge wire. Tape the wire with white tape to thicken. Dust the stalks with a little darker champagne. Encourage the seedheads to curve gently.

POPPY SEEDHEADS

Paste
Pale grey

•

Cutters
Fine calyx (527)

•

Wire
24-gauge, 28-gauge

•

Tape
White

•

Dusts
*Grey, champagne,
cream, white*

♣ Make some round balls from paste. Convert these to a pear shape. Hook the 24-gauge wire and either moisten the end of the hook with egg white or heat it with a cigarette lighter until it is red hot. Insert it into the base of the seedhead, thus fastening it in firmly. Create a very slender neck, with a very sharply flattened base to the seedhead.

♣ Form a cage with five 28-gauge wires cut in half. Insert the narrow end of the pear shape into the cage and, making sure the wires are evenly spaced, squeeze gently to mark the indentations. Remove the cage and gently reinforce the marks with a dresden foot, giving shallow depressions where the wire marks were. Gently pinch the raised sections to form ridges. Make sure the top of the pear shape is very slender. Cut off a small piece at the tip to give a flat surface. Make holes in each depression around the top

of the narrow neck of the seedhead.

♣ Roll out some paste fairly thinly. Using the fine calyx cutter, cut out two shapes. Fasten one on top of the other using a little egg white. Press together firmly. Using cranked tweezers, pinch in raised ridges on to the upper surface of the seedhead lid. Moisten the flattened tip of the seedhead with a little egg white. Fasten the lid section to it. Create a slight dome in the centre of the lid. Turn the seedhead upside down and gently lift the edges of the lid to create a slight curve. The tips of the lid may be uneven. Trim off with a sharp pair of scissors.

♣ Cut a long, straight piece of $\frac{1}{4}$-width white tape. Bind around the stem, building up a squared ridge in one place.

♣ Dust the seedhead with a little grey dust mixed with a little champagne and cream. The ridges on the lid are lighter than the lower sections of the lid.

Harvest Cake

This cake has been designed for the novice. A complete beginner could perhaps attempt just the larch twigs and cones, the beech leaves, oak leaves, acorns, and rose hips.

Medium long octagonal cake
30 × 41 cm (12 × 16¼ inch) long octagonal cake board
White or champagne sugarpaste
Orange ribbon to decorate

•

FOR THE SPRAY
2 larch twigs with cones taped together
2 sprays of honesty
1 spray of rose hips
2 sprays of Chinese lanterns
2 sprays of beech leaves (these may be the same colour or different)
2 sprays of oak leaves and acorns

♣ Cover the cake and board in white or champagne sugarpaste. Cut a template from the cake tin used. Place the template on the board where the cake will be positioned, then remove the sugarpaste from this section. If you don't want to cut out the sugarpaste, the alternative is to place the cake on a thin cake card the same size as the cake, then this may be attached to the sugarpaste-covered board. Crimp the edges neatly with a suitable crimper. Leave to dry. When the sugarpaste is dry, attach the cake to the board. Fasten the ribbon around the base of the cake, finishing the join

with a tiny bow. If you like, pipe a fine snailtrail around the cake over the lower edge of the ribbon.
♣ The larch twigs form the spine of the arrangement. Using dark brown tape, gradually add all the elements you are using to create a spray that is pleasing to the eye. I chose to use even numbers of the different dried flowers in this spray to show that if you use pieces attractively you can bend the rules a little. The more usual numbers would be odd, but the spray would then have been too large for the cake. Place the finished spray at an attractive angle on the cake.

Twigs

Wire
18-gauge, 20-gauge, 24-gauge

•

Tape
Brown

•

Dusts
Brown, nutkin brown, black, white, moss green

♣ First make some larger buds. To do this, hook a short 24-gauge wire. Cut the tape into halves. Tuck the end of the tape under the hook and then bind over the hook until you have a bud shape. Alternatively you can insert the hooks into small, slightly pointed balls of paste. With a pair of scissors, gently make the bud into three as if bracts were showing.
♣ Take a full length of 20-gauge wire and a full width of brown tape. Start taping the wire, leaving about 2.5 cm (1 inch) of tape protruding at the tip.

Twiddle this to a sharp point. Tape down about 5 cm (? inch) and then extend the tape about 2.5 cm (1 inch) from the wire. Fold the tape back on itself and by pulling, fasten the folded piece of tape together. Fold down one corner so it makes a triangle, fold up the lower corner so a smaller triangle results, then twist this. Tape over the lower edge so it just protrudes as a small bud. Continue doing this until you are about half-way down the wire.
♣ You can now start adding the larger buds made separately

either from tape or paste. Scatter the larger buds amongst the smaller ones, remembering that the buds are not opposites, they go spiralling down the wire fairly irregularly.

♣ About 7.5 cm (3 inch) from the end of the wire, bind in the 18-gauge wire. It helps to disguise the join if you add a cone at this junction. The cones can be put on singly. However, as they grow close together, you may wish to vary the look and bind on one cone and immediately below it fasten another cone behind the one already in place. If you wish, you can bring subsidiary twigs in from the sides and have a forked twig.

LARCH CONES

Paste
Brown

•

Cutter
Smallest blossom (F10)

•

Wire
*26-gauge brown, cut
into fifths*

•

Dusts
*Brown, nutkin brown,
black*

♣ Hook the wire. Make rounded balls of paste small enough to fit inside one of the petals. Moisten the hooked wires and insert them into the balls of paste. Roll out the paste until it is fairly fine and cut out shapes with the blossom cutter. Using a dresden tool, firmly frill each blossom shape. You will need three layers for each larch cone. Place the frilled blossom on a foam pad and press the small ball of a dog bone tool into each petal, cupping firmly.

♣ Moisten the centre and one petal of the first layer. Pull the wired knob through the centre of the layer, and cup the first petal around the knob. Going from side to side, repeat this process. Do not spiral the bracts.

♣ For the second layer, repeat the frilling and cupping, but only moisten the centre of the layer. Pull the first layer into the centre and just gather up the bracts fairly firmly. The third layer is the same.

♣ Now grasp the finished cone between your fingers and squash it gently. You do not want the cone to look like a badly made rose, and the squashing tends to wipe out any tendency in this direction! Dust the cone with a combination of the brown, nutkin brown and black dusts. When dry, dip the cone in a ½-glaze. Leave to dry.

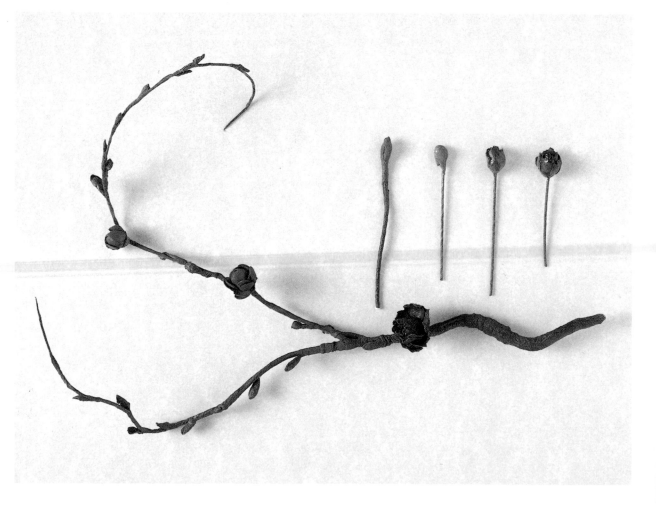

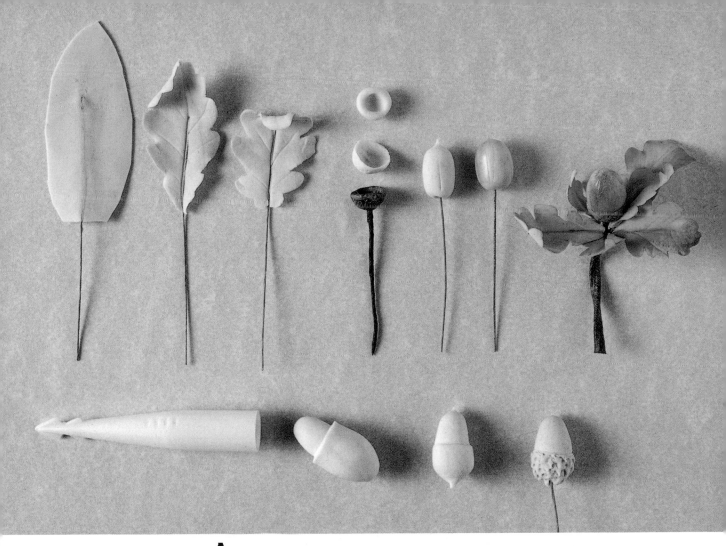

Acorns

Paste
Pale cream, using chestnut, brown, with a touch of green

•

Dusts
Champagne, cream, moss green, nutkin brown

•

Wire
26-gauge brown wire or 26-gauge wire taped with $\frac{1}{4}$-width brown tape (wires should be rather short)

♣ Take a marble-size piece of paste and roll it into a neat, crack-free barrel shape. Hook the end of the wire, moisten the end of the hook with egg white and insert into the paste. Pinch a very sharp point on to the tip of the acorn. Create striations on the surface of the acorn with the scriber and veiner. Dust lightly with champagne dust with a dash of cream and moss green. Set aside to dry completely. Glaze with a full glaze. Set aside to dry once more.

♣ To make the cup, take a piece of paste about a third to a quarter the size of the acorn itself. Roll into a small ball. Using the smaller end of a dog bone tool, make an indentation in the ball of paste. Gently rotate the dog bone tool, cupping the paste. Do not make the cup too deep. Once you have achieved the shape you want, gently thin down the edge of the cup so that it looks as though it is very fine. Using the larger end of the dog bone tool, roll the surface of the cup on to a nutmeg grater to give some texturing. Dust the cup with brown, nutkin brown and moss green. Glaze the cup with a $\frac{1}{4}$-glaze. Attach to the nut with a little egg white.

♣ The nuts are usually fastened together in pairs. To create greater realism you can make some cups without nuts. To do this make the cup as before, but using a very small hook heated with a cigarette lighter, burn the wire into the cup. The inside of the cup is a dark, glossy brown with a pale creamy spot in the centre. This is added after the wire has been fastened in place and covers the spot where the wire is attached. Be careful to fasten this piece in tightly, rolling the dog bone tool around the inside of the cup to ensure a tight bond.

♣ The inside of the acorn cup is very glossy – glaze with a full glaze.

♣ A friend of mine showed me a very simple way of making an acorn. This is very quick and easy to do so makes an excellent commercial decoration. Using a Wilton flower pick and a sausage of paste just narrower than the mouth of the flower pick, insert the paste into the about 1 cm ($\frac{1}{2}$ inch) depending on the shape you prefer for your acorn. Gently push some more paste just over the tip of the pick forming a slight ridge. Remove from the pick. Pat the ridge flat against the acorn, pinching the tip to a sharp point. Gently roll the sausage of paste between your forefingers, cutting off the excess paste. This should be about a third the length of the acorn itself. The cup can be textured with a pair of tweezers or a nutmeg grater. Wire can be inserted if required.

♣ Made in kirsh-flavoured marzipan with the cup part dipped in chocolate, they make a very quick, simple gift.

ROSE HIPS

Paste
Orangey red, greeny brown

•

Cutters
Smallest calyx (406) or R15

•

Stamens
Fine black

•

Wire
24-gauge green

•

Dusts
Red, nutkin brown, black

♣ Take a medium sized ball of orangey red paste and form as you prefer (some rose hips are barrel shaped, some are round, some are tyre shaped and some are pear shaped). Cut the wires into $\frac{1}{4}$ lengths. Hook the wire. Insert the wire into the paste, fastening it in place either with egg white or by heating the end of the wire with a cigarette lighter.

♣ Roll out some of the browny green paste and cut out sepals using the small calyx cutter. Soften the sepals with a dog bone tool, then distort them slightly with the veining tool. Attach to the pointed end of the hip with a little egg white. Make a hole into the ball of paste with a celstick. Insert a cut-off stamen into the hole, allowing it to protrude slightly. Arrange the sepals unevenly.

♣ Dust the hip a good red. Dust the sepals a deeper shade with the nutkin brown and black. Allow to dry completely. Dip the hips into full glaze and allow to dry again.

♣ The hips can either be used individually in arrangements, or wired into their natural groupings.

Paste
Very pale cream (using chestnut or white)

•

Cutters
Bougainvillaea

•

Wire
26-gauge white

•

Tape
White

•

Dusts
Champagne, cream, nutkin brown, Mother-of-pearl
Paste colour dark brown

Purple dust (for the leaves) is made by blending 2 portions of plum dust with 1 red, 1 cornflower blue and 1 nutkin brown.

HONESTY

♣ *Seedhead*: Cut the wire into thirds. Tie a knot in each wire about 4 cm (1½ inch) from one end of the wire. These knots should be pulled very tight indeed.

♣ Cut a piece of white tape into ¼ widths with a tape shredder. Taking one piece of wire, cover it with tape leaving about 2.5 cm (1 inch) of tape overlapping at one end. With a sharp pair of scissors, cut this in half lengthwise. Twiddle each of the two halves, being careful not to pull them off. When they are in threads, gently curve them towards one another like a pair of brackets. This piece of wire forms the top section of a completed stem of seedheads.

♣ To make the seedheads themselves, roll out the paste very thinly using a grooved rolling pin or grooved board. Cut out the shapes, leaving the groove in place. Insert a moistened wire into the shape, having the nodule positioned just below the junction of the paste

and the wire. Very carefully pinch the thickened tip of the shape to a very sharp point, then roll it very gently between your fingers so that it extends about 1 cm (½ inch). (This will be very delicate when it is dry so be careful not to bump it.) Using a dog bone tool, gently soften the paste on a foam pad. On this occasion you are NOT working on the edge of the shape. There is a rim to the seedhead where the veins lie, and the centre of the seedhead is more delicate than the edge. Press very gently on the inner section of the seedhead on either side of the wire so that slight indentations are created. It is at this point that you can remove any groove that may remain above the end of the wire and the tip of the seedhead.

♣ Dust this seedhead immediately after making it while the tip is still fairly flexible. First dust the stem a fairly deep browny cream (on some plants it is quite a dark brown so decide for yourself which you prefer). Paint the edge of the seedpod a browny cream. Use a medium

Paste
Pale melon, holly/ivy

•

Cutters
*Quick fuchsia skirt
(537), smallest size,
anthurium cutter*

•

Stamens
Miniature yellow

•

Wire
*28-gauge, 26-gauge,
24-gauge*

•

Tape
White

•

Dusts
*Plum, cornflower blue,
violet, primrose yellow,
moss green, mixed dark
green made of equal
proportions of jade, apple
green, moss green, nutkin
brown, a touch of black*

Leaves: Roll pale
green paste on a
grooved board or
pin. Cut out using
veiners or a template.
Insert moistened 26
or 24-gauge wire into
central vein, place
between veiners and
squeeze. Remove and
flick away excess
paste, soften on a
foam pad. Place the
leaf over shaped
foam.
When firm not
brittle, dust using
apple, moss and
jade green, nutkin
brown, purple.

paintbrush loaded with the colour you prefer, and with the side of the brush paint the colour in place. If you try to use the tip of the brush it is far too easy to get smudges on the surface of the seedhead.

♣ Paint between three and six very fine lines from the edge of the seedhead about a third of the way into the centre; these are the veins which connected the seed to the arterial system. Turn over the seedhead and, holding it up against the light so you can see where the lines are, repeat on the second side. Carefully paint the long point at the tip with the dark colour as well. Dust the seedhead with the pearl dust.

Flower: Attach five fine yellow stamens to a 28-gauge wire using $\frac{1}{4}$-width tape.

♣ To make the buds, attach a very small piece of pale melon paste to the 28-gauge wire, making the bud slender and pointed. Give it a long narrow taper on to the wire. The calyx is narrow at the top edge, widening slightly towards the base where it cuts off sharply. Mark a strong line down the centre of the calyx. From the front it looks like an inverted, elongated slender heart. It is flattened from side to side.

♣ Dust the tip of the bud a purply colour. The calyx should be dusted a fairly deep green and then glazed with a $\frac{1}{2}$-glaze.

♣ To make the flower, take a small piece of pale melon paste. Make a fine pedicel and roll out the paste very finely. Cut out the petals. Between the petals cut out a thin wedge of paste, making the petals more individual. Soften the edges of the paste and gently vein the petals with a scriber. Open the throat of the flower with a celstick or skewer. Moisten the wire just below the stamens and pull through into the throat of the flower.

♣ Dust the petals a purply colour, fading to a pale melon near the stamens. Very carefully paint in radiating lines of darker purple on to each petal. Each flower has a calyx made as described for the bud.

Unpeeled seedheads: If you are creating a living plant as opposed to using the seedheads in a dried arrangement, it is nice to have some seedheads where the outer skins and seeds are still in place. To do this repeat the instructions as before, but on one or two of the seedheads add a few dark brown, small, flat seeds to the piece. It is important to note that the seeds should be attached to both sides of the seedhead, but there should not be two seeds attached to the same vein. Scatter half on one side of the seedhead and half on the other, each seed having its own vein. An extremely thin layer of paste is then attached over the seeds on both sides of the seedhead. Slight moistening of the thickened edge is all that is needed. Cut off the excess paste and gently curl back a little paste at the base of the seedhead to allow a seed or two to be seen.

♣ Allow this to dry slightly before decorating the outside. The outer layers of the seedhead are darker in colour and rather grubby looking. Using an old toothbrush or stencil brush. Start with a fairly pale colour petal dust mixed with a liquid and with a box behind it flick the colour on to the seedhead. You can gradually darken the splotches as you like.

OAK AND BEECH LEAVES

OAK LEAVES
Paste
Cream

•

Cutter
Oak leaf

•

Veiner
Oak leaf (OL 1, 2, 3, 4)

•

Wire
*26-gauge brown,
28-gauge taped with
brown tape*

•

Dusts
*Champagne, cream,
skintone, egg yellow,
orange, red, brown,
nutkin brown, green,
plum black*

BEECH LEAVES
Paste
Pale cream

•

Cutters
*A template of a beech leaf
or a large rose leaf cutter*

•

Veiner
Beech leaf or rose leaf

•

Wire
26-gauge brown, ¼ lengths

•

Dusts
*Champagne, cream,
skintone, brown, nutkin
brown, red, nasturtium
for common beech. Plum,
red, brown, nutkin brown
with a touch of black for
copper beech*

OAK LEAVES
♣ Roll out the paste to medium thickness on a non-stick board. Rub a little cornflour under and over the paste, then using a grooved rolling pin, roll out a length of paste. Cut out the leaves with the oak leaf cutter. Soften the edges with a dog bone tool. Insert moistened wires into the ridge left at the centre of the leaf. Shape some of the leaves as if they are curling up by rolling the tips around a small celstick.

♣ Dust the leaves with champagne, cream, skintone, egg yellow, orange, red, brown and nutkin brown dust in different combinations. The last part of the leaf to go brown is around the central vein. If you like, dust in a little green here. Allow the leaves to dry in many varied shapes. Glaze them with a ¼-glaze. Allow to dry and then wire the leaves into clusters with three small pale brown buds in the centre. Buds are made by rolling tiny balls of paste on to 28-gauge wire, rolling the tips to a point and dusting with brown. Glaze with a ½ glaze.

BEECH LEAVES
♣ Roll out the paste very thinly on a grooved board, or fairly thinly and then again with the grooved rolling pin to create the central vein.

♣ Cut out the leaves, moisten the end of a wire and insert into the thickened centre line of the leaf. The further you insert the wire, the less chance there is of breakage. Using a dog bone tool, soften the edge of the leaves on a pad of foam.

Pressed Flowers

Making pressed flowers in sugar requires a lot of discipline! For once it is not necessary to spend so much time creating movement and life from a piece of flat paste.

To create the effect of a pressed flower picture you must avoid the odd little lift here and there. It may improve the flower slightly if it were for anything else, but here 'flat is beautiful'. It is so easy to loose the effect we are striving to achieve.

Having mastered this element, the next thing to consider is which flowers are most appropriate. I have found that it is best to avoid anything which has raised stamens in the centre. Wild roses may look good pressed, but in trying to create the effect in sugar they loose a lot of their delicacy.

A list of some of the flowers I prefer using is as follows: birdsfoot ivy, maidenhair fern, ground ivy, pansies, violas, single fuchsias, cranes bill, daisies, speckled abutilon, potentilla, red campion, ivy-leaved toadflax, primrose, wood sorrel, forget-me-not, ferns, hydranga, small rose leaves, Japanese maple, silverweed, thalictrum. One can then just create 'fantasy flowers' using any cutters you like. We don't need to be restricted by flowers that grow naturally, we are just creating shapes. Maidenhair fern gives a lovely light look to a picture. You don't have to wire each of the little leaflets, the stems can be done with pieces of thread which gives the fineness you want without the bulk – your

other alternative is to paint or draw in the very fine stems. Keep it on a small scale – you will require a few larger components, but in general you will find small cutters give you the most satisfactory results.

In my search for the best effects I have assembled a rather mixed bag of cutters that fulfil most of the criteria I have mentioned. The most delicate leaves by and large are achieved using some of the Zimbabwean very fine leaf cutters.

The next find I made was that of a range of Australian cutters which are ideal for the job in hand. Naturally I also use a cross section of other manufacturers' cutters, but on this occasion these small fine cutters are absolutely marvellous. Veining is important. A lot more interesting designs can be created if there is good veining.

The next thing to remember is not to use the usual depth of colour we normally strive to achieve. Pressing flowers has the effect of fading them to a certain degree. You will create far more realism if you resist the urge to 'just add a little more colour'. If you do so, the picture won't look realistic. The best bet is to get some books on pressed flowers out of the library and keep them to hand while you work on these projects. Naturally in a book of this type I can only give you a

taste of this fascinating branch of sugarcraft. The greatest compliment you can receive is the reaction . . . 'well I'd never have thought it was sugar!'

If you are making a picture for a frame, you could also cheat a little and use some dried asparagus fern. I would not use anything inedible like this on a card, plaque or cake, but if it is to be stuck on to card and displayed under glass on a wall, a little cheating is permissible.

Working on plaques, cards and cakes, make sure your background is completely dry, otherwise the flowers may become buried in the back-ground. I have found it easier to assemble the picture if the flowers and leaves are 'leather hard' – firm but not brittle. There will be less breakage and they are more easily

arranged as you can lift a petal to tuck a leaf underneath it and so on.

When designing a pressed flower picture, first think about colour. Choose flowers and leaves that are in the same tone range, or are complementary.

The next task is to sketch out on paper the shape you want your piece to take. Look at the shape of the picture, card or plaque and choose a design you feel will look attractive.

You then need to make the flowers you will be using. If you are using pansies or violas you make them similarly to the way you would normally, except you do not have a wire.

Paste
Pale green

•

Cutters
*Small calyx (406),
rose petal (279, 280) or
pansy (78, 79, 80)*

•

Veiner
Medium poppy petal

•

Dusts
Muted colours

PANSY OR VIOLA

❧ The method for making these two flowers is very similar, the only difference being that the pansy petals are much more rounded, the whole flower has an almost circular appearance, and, of course, it is larger than the viola.

❧ Using pale green paste, cut out a flat calyx shape with a small calyx cutter. As it won't be seen there is no point in shaping it.

❧ Next roll out pale melon paste and cut out the petals, using rose petal cutters. Cut out five petals. Stretch the lower petal by frilling more briskly with a cocktail stick. Roll the edges with a cocktail stick or celstick as you would normally, but remember to keep this to a minimum. You only want to soften the edges, not

actually frill them as you will get ugly creases when you flatten them.

❧ Using a medium poppy veiner, vein the petals, or use a cocktail stick to mark in some veins. Position the two back petals on the calyx, add the middle petals and then the large lower petal. Remember to position the point of the lower petal high up between the middle petals. Using the dresden foot, press down firmly. This will bond the layers of petals together and to the backing calyx, it will also force the point of the lower petal to form the 'eyebrows'. If they are not noticeable enough, use a pair of tweezers to sharpen this feature.

❧ Use very muted colours to dust the petals.

♣ Place the flower between the layers of a plastic file cover and using something flat in your hand, press down evenly on to the flower to flatten it. Take it out, touch up the colouring and cut off any pieces which are out of place. Paint in the dark markings and set it aside until you have made as many flowers as you need.

♣ If you want to make some violas or pansies as though they are a side view, you will have to cut the piece representing the spur freehand and arrange it behind the petals. Remember you are just creating an illusion of a pressed flower. If you work joins with tip of your dresden tool you can make most joins disappear, particularly if you position the petals carefully.

POTENTILLA

Make these flowers in different sizes. Roll out mid green paste and cut a calyx using a small calyx cutter (R15). On top of this place a flower, cut with a blossom cutter (F9 or F10) from very finely rolled paste, the edges very gently softened. Place the petals between the points of the sepals. You should be able to see some of the green of the sepals between the petals. Moisten the centre with egg white and gently add sugartex, coloured semolina etc. to create the stamens. This should be neatly done as it spoils the effect if the stamens are allowed to scatter over the petals. Very gently dust in the desired colouring.

FUCHSIA

Roll a very fine tube of paste. Roll out the paste at the base and cut out the sepals using a fuchsia cutter. Soften the edges of the sepals, fold the piece in half so you can see all four sepals and, placing it between the folds of a plastic file cover, flatten it. Cut out four small rose petals, carefully lift the upper two sepals and arrange the petals where they are wanted. The long stamens should be moistened with a little egg white and fastened in place as well. The leaves are made using a Japanese maple cutter. Cut out a shape and then cut the various leaflets apart. With suitable veining and colouring they look most effective.

PRIMROSE

Some primrose flowers can be presented as just being the face of the flower. Using a primrose cutter (F3, F3M), cut out the flat shape of the flower. Soften the edges, decorate as for the actual flower, make a hole in the centre of the flower as though the tube was there and arrange it as you want it. If you are presenting a side version you have to cut the flower out as one would normally, but bearing in mind the paste will spread when you squash it, make the tube narrower than seems right. Arrange the petals so you can see all five of them. Cut a small green piece of paste freehand in the shape the calyx appears illustrated in a pressed flower book.

FORGET-ME-NOT

Use fine piping tubes to cut out the tiny pieces which represent the pressed buds. Remember that the buds of a forget-me-not are pink. Paint in the stem, or use a thread moistened with egg white and stuck in place to represent the stem. Cut the little blossoms flat and decorate them as for the face of the flower.

Pastillage
White (see page 102)

•

Paste
*Pale pink, pale cream,
white, mid green,
pale green*

•

Cutters
*Australian fern leaf,
Zimbabwean fine leaf,
small plunger, small
blossom (F10), small
metal stephanotis (568)*

•

Dusts
*Pale pink, silver lustre,
yellow folk art paint
Black icing pen, tip
slightly sharpened*

PASTILLAGE
Pressed Flower Card

This makes a lovely and original gift for a friend on a birthday or other special occasion. If wished, a name or simple message could be added with the black icing pen.

♣ Roll out the pastillage very thinly and cut out a card shape measuring about 18 cm (7 inch) long by 10 cm (4 inch) deep using a pizza wheel to prevent pulling. Set aside to dry on a flat surface lightly dusted with cornflour, turning regularly. Make sure the edges are neat. If there are any small imperfections they may be removed by very gently filing with an emery board.

♣ Using the icing pen, draw a fine line about 7.5 cm ($\frac{3}{8}$ inch) from the edge of the card, forming a frame.

Cut out small and medium fern leaves using pale green paste and form into three fern leaf sprays. Add other leaves between these, coming in to the centre of the card. Use different colour green paste to add to the picture. Decorate the centre of the card with pale pink, cream and white flowers. Paint small yellow centres into the flowers using the yellow folk paint. Although pressed flowers should be very flat, use a little artistic licence to create a slightly less formal look to the card.

✿ Stand the two halves of the card on the lower edge, prop them in position and stick the two halves together using a little royal icing.

Trinket Bowl

As pressed flowers have not previously appeared in a cake decorating book I wanted to use them on a cake, not just on cards or wall decorations, and this seemed an attractive way of using this skill.

✿ Cover the silver cake board with the dark green sugarpaste and allow to dry. When decorated with the flowers and swags, this will form the lid of the trinket bowl.

✿ Place the cake on the thin board. Build up the side of the cake with marzipan to give the desired bowl shape. Coat with the white sugarpaste and allow to dry. To avoid the underside of the bowl from being flattened in an unattractive manner, place the cake on a tin or weight smaller than the diameter of the cake.

✿ Mould three 2.2 cm ($\frac{7}{8}$ inch) tudor buttons from pastillage and set aside to dry. Paint them with brilliant silver food colouring moistened with a little gin, vodka or cooking oil when dry. If you use the cooking oil a higher shine results, but it takes a long time for the colour to set completely; smudging may occur. The smudges may, however, be painted over when the decorative pieces are in place.

✿ Mould six 7 cm ($2\frac{3}{4}$ inch) swags from pastillage and set aside to dry. Paint them with brilliant silver food colouring when dry.

✿ Mark a 12 cm ($4\frac{1}{2}$ inch) circle in the centre of the dark green sugarpasted board. Carefully paint this with silver food colouring.

✿ Cut out the leaves and background flowers with appropriate cutters in groups of three. Colour them as illustrated. The silvery effect is achieved by dusting the fine leaves with silver lustre colour. This is best done while the leaves are newly cut out and quite flexible, so you do not break off any of the tiny pieces which become very brittle when dry.

✿ All the flowers and leaves should be stuck in place with a little gum glue or egg white while they are still flexible. Remember

18 cm (7 inch) round cake, at least 7.5 cm (3 inch) deep
18 cm (7 inch) thin round hardboard cake board
15 cm (6 inch) silver cake board
125 g (4 oz) dark green sugarpaste
1.25 kg (2½ lb) white sugarpaste
Pastillage (see page 102)
Tudor button mould 2.2 cm (⅞ inch)
Swag mould 7 cm (2¾ inch) long
Brilliant silver food colouring
Pale green, mid green, pale yellow, off white and white flower paste
Silver luster dust
Royal icing

•

SPECIAL CUTTERS FOR LID
Zimbabwean fine leaf cutters
Australian fern leaf cutters
Australian tiny white flower cutter
Central leaf cut from a Japanese maple cutter (JM3)
Small blossom cutter (F10)
Metal pansy cutter (78, 79, 80)

to dust the pansy with muted colours for a natural look. Pressed flowers tend to loose some of their colour so the effect is more realistic when muted tones are used.

♣ To assemble the cake; divide the circumference of the base into three and position the tudor buttons so that they protrude slightly from underneath the cake. Allow to dry properly.

♣ Cut a circle of sugarpaste 5 mm ($\frac{1}{4}$ inch) deep and 14 cm ($5\frac{3}{4}$ inch) diameter. Attach this to the top of the cake and allow to dry properly.

♣ Divide the circumference of the lid into six. Attach the silver painted swags to the upper edge of the lid using a little royal icing, gum glue or egg white. Pipe six beads of white royal icing between the swags. Carefully dust with a little silver lustre colour.

♣ Stick the lid in place on top of the cake.

♣ Place the now completed trinket bowl on a large oval board covered with a toning piece of velvet (see photograph) to complete the picture.

BONSAI

Before you embark on making
any of the bonsai trees in this
chapter, spend some time looking
at pictures of the real thing.
Notice that the flowers and fruit
are large in proportion to the tree
itself – it can take a while to get
used to this phenomenon.
Of the three projects that follow,
the Wisteria Bonsai is the most
difficult and time-consuming.

Bonsai

One of the most interesting things about bonsai is that although branches, twigs and leaves are all in miniature, the flowers and fruit, being the reproductive parts, are not.

Bonsai is an ancient form of Chinese and Japanese art.

'The word is taken from the Chinese words bon-sai, which means a potted tree. However, merely having a tree in a pot does not necessarily make it a bonsai. A bonsai is an artistic replica of a natural tree in miniature form. It exists only in a pot or container. It is essentially a work of art . . . and is above all a picture or illusion of a real tree.'

This extract is from the book *Bonsai – The Art of Growing and Keeping Miniature Trees* by Peter Chan, published by Quintet Publishing Ltd 1986, and is a very good description of this very complicated art form. I will not try to describe all the different styles there are. The topic is far too complex to try to break down in a few short sentences. One of the most exciting aspects of bonsai is the lovely movement you can get into your work.

Many bonsai trees are very gnarled, and this is encouraged by growers who deliberately damage the bark to cause interesting patterns. Try to recreate this in your work.

Some bonsai are planted next to or over rocks. More often than not the rocks chosen for this purpose are volcanic rocks which have a lot of holes, hollows and crevices.

Good bonsai also often have strong exposed roots to add visual interest. The branches radiate around the trunk. 'A good analogy for the right arrangement of branches is a spiral staircase.' (*The Complete Book of Bonsai* by Harry Tomlinson, Dorling Kindersley.)

Bearing all this in mind you can now set about creating your own bonsai, which may take many hours of work with all the leaves, buds and flowers that must be made before you can begin to put it all together. At least we can create a sugar bonsai in hours rather than the many years it takes to make a real one!

This weird looking object is a root for a bonsai. It looks so strange as the upper edge has been tapered to fit alongside a section of the trunk.

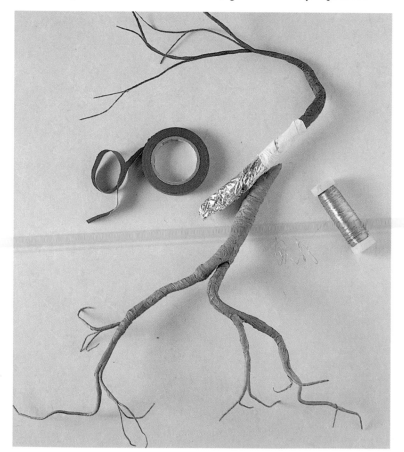

Flowering Cherry Bonsai

About 30 leaves in two or three sizes
25 buds
10–15 small tight flowers
20–25 full flowers
18 and 20-gauge wires
Olive green and brown tape
Floristry wire
Brown, nutkin brown and black dusts
Floristry staysoft
Confectioners' glaze

In typical oriental style the rather thick, gnarled branches of this piece contrast beautifully with the delicate pink petals of each gracefully drooping flower.

❧ Tape all the wires with olive green tape cut into quarters. Fasten the flowers into clusters of between five and ten buds and flowers, leaving the wires about 6–7.5 cm (2½–3 inch) long. Now back these clusters with a cluster of two or three leaves. These clusters should each be taped on to the end of a 20-gauge wire.

❧ Immediately start building up bulk on the twigs, using full width brown tape. The first three clusters do not have very thick stems, but do remember to thicken them for a good length of the wire as it helps to build up the bulk in the stem. Stagger the first three clusters. The second one is taped in about 2.5 cm (1 inch) down from the first one. Leave a gap of 3.5 cm (1½ inch) to the next one. From this point, start bulking out the branch with strips of kitchen paper between the layers of tape.

❧ Form another three branches similar to the first one, padding them as you go. Gradually bind them together on to two 18-gauge wires. Remember to spiral the branches around the main trunk, thickening the trunk as you go. Cherry trees have very rough, gnarled bark. Once you have taped two branches together firmly and have padded the section as much as you need, bind some narrow folded kitchen foil over the padding, wrinkling it as much as you can. Roughen the bark by continuing to tape over the section but twisting the tape into a thread. Bind this up and down the section, causing ridges and lumps. Tape one layer of full width tape over this to disguise the ridges, but not eliminate the rough look. Gradually taper the

padding and tape as you reach the desired length for the stem.

🍀 Using a long 18-gauge wire cut into three, make the roots as described earlier in the chapter. Using silver florist's wire, bind the three roots together firmly. The roots should each be 7.5–13 cm (3–5 inch) long; longer if they are to be bound over a rock.

🍀 Bind the roots to the trunk, fitting the tapering trunk wire between or alongside the root wires. Bind this tightly with floristry wire. Now bind paper and tape over the junction until it is not noticeable. It should feel very secure. Bind the tape between the roots as you would bandage fingers.

🍀 Once it is all joined firmly, remember to create the rough texture of the bark by taping with threaded tape. Cover this with one layer of tape. Using a fork, distressing tool, scriber, craft knife and texturing brush, cause some more roughness to the bark. Dust the tape with brown, nutkin brown and black dust. The roots should be a little lighter in colour. Hold the trunk and force it to bend as you want.

🍀 Use floristry staysoft in the bonsai pot you have chosen. If you are using rock see that the roots cling to it securely. Add staysoft until you are sure it won't wobble. Arrange each twig and branch into pleasing shapes, considering its appearance from every angle. Cover the staysoft with the soil mixture described above. Spray the trunk sparingly with an aerosol confectioners' glaze to give it a little gloss.

FLOWERING CHERRY

Paste
Pale pink, pale green

•

Cutters
Blossom (F10), small calyx (406), simple leaf (228, 230, 231)

•

Veiner
Cherry leaf

•

Stamens
Miniature, pale yellow

•

Wire
28-gauge, 26-gauge

•

Dusts
Fuchsia, pink, plum, apple green, moss green

🍀 Fasten five short stamens to the end of a 26-gauge wire. Roll out the pink paste very thinly and cut three shapes for each flower using the blossom cutter.

🍀 *Layer 1*: Frill the edge of each petal with a dresden tool. Turn the petal over on to a foam pad and cup it with the small ball of a dog bone tool. Moisten the centre and pull the stamens through the petals. Gently arrange the petals and allow to firm up with the head hanging down so that the petals cluster around the stamens.

🍀 *Layer 2*: Frill the edge of each petal with the dresden tool, then soften the petals a little further with a cocktail stick. Repeat the rest as for the first layer.

🍀 *Layer 3*: Repeat as for the second layer, but frill the edges of the petal more firmly.

🍀 To make the calyx, make a small hip with pale green paste. A Mexican hat board would help get the sizes even. With your fingers flatten the paste, then roll it out finely. Cut out the calyx.

🍀 Place on the foam pad with the hip upwards. With a very fine ball tool, gently stroke each sepal from the tip to the centre so that it curls up gently. Moisten the back of the last petal slightly near the wire. Pull the wire through the hip and fasten in place making sure that the sepals come at the junction of the last layer of petals. When the flowers are firm but not brittle, dust them to the colour you prefer.

BUD

♣ Take a very small ball of
paste. Make a very small hook at
the end of a 28-gauge wire.
Moisten and insert into the ball
of paste. Pinch the tip of the bud
to a sharp point.

♣ Make a cage with five
28-gauge wires. Insert the bud
into the cage point first. Spread
the wires evenly. Squeeze the
wires together tightly until they
bite firmly into the paste.
Remove the wires and allow the
buds to dry.

♣ Make the calyx as for the
flower. Moisten the back of
the bud and pull the wire
through the hip of the calyx.
Dust lightly to tone with the
flowers.

LEAVES

♣ In many cases, the leaves of
the flowering cherry are a rich
burgundy colour when they first
appear. I decided that for the
purposes of my tree, green leaves
would be preferable.

♣ Roll out the paste on a
grooved board or with a grooved
rolling pin. Cut out the leaves
with a simple leaf cutter,
remembering to turn the cutters
over from time to time so that
you get the leaves turning in
opposite directions.

♣ Moisten the tip of a 28-gauge
wire and insert it into the central
vein of the leaf. Soften the edges
of the leaf with a dog bone tool.
Impress the veins on to the leaf,
reinforce the central vein by
pinching between your fingers,
soften the leaves slightly by
bending them a little. Set aside to
firm up.

♣ Dust the leaves with a little
apple and moss green with a hint
of fuchsia at the edges. Glaze
with $\frac{1}{2}$-glaze and set aside to
dry.

There is not much
movement at the
edge of these leaves
so they appear a
little stiff.

BONSAI

Wisteria Bonsai

Racemes of flowers
8–10 compound leaves
18- and 20-gauge wires
White or pale beige tape
Kitchen foil
Kitchen paper
Fine floristry binding
wire
Floristry staysoft

'Plant' this taller bonsai in a deeper pot so that more staysoft can be used without it being too obvious.

To allow for the long hanging racemes and compound leaves, the wisteria bonsai will need more roots to spread out to take the weight of the completed piece.

❧ Make three to four racemes of between ten and fifteen buds and about fifteen flowers. Divide racemes and leaves into three different sized branches.
❧ Tape 18-gauge wires, adding kitchen foil to thicken. Tape two roots together about 8–10 cm ($3\frac{1}{2}$–4 inch) from the tip. Repeat with another pair. The last two roots keep separate. Once you have bound the roots together tightly with the florist's wire, divide the wires into two uneven groups. Thicken, elongate and tape these two sections separately. Twine and bind them tightly around one another. If the stem does not yet feel thick enough, add another twining section. Gradually taper them towards the top, where the branches will be added. Radiate the branches fairly evenly.
❧ Dust the stem until it is a pale beige/grey colour. Use a toothbrush to splatter marks along the pale bark, being careful to protect the leaves and flowers with kitchen paper.
❧ Firmly work the roots into the staysoft in the pot.

Paste
Pale melon, pale green

•

Cutters
Rose petal (79, 80), tiny blossom plunger, smallest plunger blossom, single petal daisy (89, 90, 91)

•

Wire
32-gauge, 28-gauge, 26-gauge

•

Tape
Nile green

•

Dusts
Primrose yellow, lemon yellow, lavender, cornflower blue, violet, white, apple green, vine green

WISTERIA

❧ The racemes of the wisteria are made up of a great number of individual buds and blossoms. The leaves, too, are compound and also need a great number of pieces!
❧ The buds are very simply made from tiny to small pieces of pale melon paste. Each bud looks like a small keel with a tiny calyx in place. These should be formed on the end of a 32-gauge wire.
❧ The partly open buds are made from a keel with a pair of petals. Roll and cut out a rose petal in pale melon paste, cutting a long, fairly narrow wedge out of the centre of the petal. Soften and curve the two resulting arms to gently enclose the keel.

❧ To make the standard, roll out the pale melon paste very finely and cut out a rose petal. Transfer it to a foam pad, soften the edge and mark a strong line down the centre of the petal. On either side of the line, gently stroke the petal with a dog bone tool from the broad end to the narrow tip to make it curl gently. Moisten the tip of the petal and attach it to the first two layers, lifting it gently away from them so a small gap results. Set them aside to dry. Add the small calyx made from the plunger blossom cutter.
❧ To make the flowers, repeat the above process for the first two layers (keel and wings), using larger rose petal cutters. It should be noted that the keel is hardly visible on these flowers from the front. The keel is almost

Wisteria bark is very ridged and wrinkled and does not taper evenly up the stem. Lumps and bumps can be formed with the foil before taping over them. If it needs more interest, keep adding lumps and bumps until you achieve the required effect.

When working the roots into the staysoft, make a mossy effect using a cheap nylon strainer and some softened paste.

completely covered by the wings. For the larger standard, the process is similar except you must stroke the petal strongly on either side of the central line so the petal curls backwards. With a cocktail stick or a small celstick, roll the side edges of the petal backwards as well. Moisten the tip of the petal, fasten it in place, supported by a foam scrap. When it is set but not brittle, add the calyx.

❧ Dust the flowers and then wire all the buds and flowers in place to make the raceme. Tape the racemes on to a 20-gauge wire, but do not tape the individual buds and flowers to so thick a wire otherwise they will not cascade so beautifully.

❧ This flower is greatly improved by steaming after the racemes are put together for the gentle glow typical of the flower and to lessen the 'dusty' look. The keel and the area on either side of the vein on the standard are a very pale yellow – almost white. The major part of the colour is on the wings which are quite a deep pinky mauve. The edges of the standard are lightly dusted with lavender.

LEAVES

❧ There are very few wisteria leaves on the plant at the time of flowering. They are a very pale yellowy green at this stage. Do not make the mistake of making the leaves the normal colour, or of making them profuse.

❧ Each compound leaf is made up of between nine and thirteen leaflets. Just after they unfurl they tend to droop as though needing water. A little artistic licence is allowed here! To keep the more upright shape you will want for some of the leaves, tape the individual leaflets to a 20-gauge wire.

❧ Dust the leaves attractively then dip into a $\frac{1}{4}-\frac{1}{2}$-glaze. They are fairly glossy at this time of the year.

Hazelnut Bonsai

The colours of this piece give it rather an autumnal look. Its sturdy construction contrasts strongly with the delicacy of the previous project. If wished, some volcanic rock can be tightly packed into the bonsai pot for added effect.

7 hazelnuts
36 hazel leaves
18- and 20-gauge wires
Pale beige tape
Floristry staysoft
Bonsai pot of your choice
Kitchen paper
Silver florist's wire

♣ Tape and thicken three ½-length 18-gauge wires to make the roots. Kitchen paper can be cut into 2.5 cm (1 inch) strips and used between layers of tape. The roots should be naturally tapered in both directions, leaving a length of unthickened wire at one end. Set these aside.

♣ Using two 20-gauge wires and a cluster of nuts, create two branches for your tree. Arrange the leaves alternately, spiralling around the stems.

♣ Using 20-gauge wire again, create three more twigs without hazelnuts.

♣ Fasten one of the 20-gauge wires with a cluster of nuts and leaves on to an 18-gauge full length wire. Bind with tape and paper as described above, gradually adding the other twigs and branches. When all have been added you will have quite a thick stem. If at any time you decide the tree is not feeling firm enough add a few more heavy wires until it feels strong and stable. Now, using silver florist's wire, add the tapering roots one at a time, joining them all at the same junction. Pad the stem and root junction with kitchen paper and tape until a natural look results.

♣ Using your scalpel, craft knife, fork, distressing tools etc., work on the surface of the bark until it looks interesting. The bark is light brown with a greeny/grey tinge, so using the petal dusts dust it to the desired shade. Now, taking the stem and roots firmly between your hands, bend the tree to the desired shape. As such heavy wire has been used a great deal of force is necessary. Hold the tree upright and see if you have achieved the shape you want. Continue like this until you are satisfied.

♣ Choose a bonsai pot. Put a lump of floristry staysoft in the base. Add the volcanic rock if using. Arrange the roots of the bonsai attractively whether or not a rock is used, packing more floristry staysoft in place around the base of the roots if needed. Make sure the whole thing is firm and steady. If you are a purist, you may prefer to use sugarpaste as the filler in the pot. Once it is set the tree won't move.

♣ Disguise the staysoft or sugarpaste with a mixture of ingredients to make it look like the peaty soil. I use a combination of petal dust, drinking chocolate, gelatine, cocoa, semolina and tea. If you choose to use the tea leaves from used tea bags you must make absolutely sure that the tea leaves are dry or they can go mouldy and ruin the whole piece. Be prepared for rude comments about strung up drying tea bags!

Paste
*Pale cream/chestnut, pale
green, holly/ivy green*

•

Cutter
*Medium to small daisy
(106)*

•

Wire
24-gauge green

•

Dusts
*Champagne, cream,
apple green, moss green*

•

Veiner

LEAVES

Paste
Pale green

•

Cutters
*Rose petals (549,
550, 551, 276)*

•

Veiner
Hazel

•

Wire
*26-gauge, some 24-gauge
(for larger leaves)*

•

Dust
*Moss green, vine green,
apple green, cream,
skintone, nutkin brown*

HAZELNUTS

♣ Take a medium-sized piece of pale cream/chestnut paste and roll it into a ball. Make it oval, but then gently pinch the upper edges to make them narrower than the base. The pinching may be taken about a third of the way down the sides. The base should be quite rounded. Insert a hooked 24-gauge wire into the broad base. Pinch the tip of the nut to a sharp point. Mark striations on to the nut using a scriber and a veiner. Dust the nut with champagne, a little cream and a little moss green dust.

♣ Set aside and allow to dry completely. As these nuts grow very close together it is wise to fasten two nuts tightly together while they dry so you can nestle them together once the husk has been added. Dip the nut into a ¾-glaze to give a moderately high shine. Set aside to dry again.

♣ Roll out some pale green paste until it is very thin. Cut out with the daisy cutter; elongate the central petal on either side and elongate slightly less the two petals on either side of this, up to a point joining the petals together. Frill all these petals with the veiner so that they become jagged and uneven. Moisten the centre of the daisy shape with egg white and attach to the dried, glazed nut. The shortest petals should go to the sides of the nut, where the pinched shoulders slope down. Some of the husk should be quite close to the nut but do curve back some of the husk in attractive curves. Dust the husk with a little moss green dust, and also a little cream.

♣ As the nut has already been glazed you do not need to dip the husk-covered nut into further glaze. Set the dust on the husk by holding it over a steaming kettle spout for a couple of seconds. This gets rid of the dusty look.

LEAVES

♣ Roll out the paste fairly thinly either on the grooved board or using the grooved rolling pin. Cut out leaves with the cutters. Insert a moistened 26-gauge wire into the central vein of the leaf. Press the rolled out paste on to the veiner, making sure that the line of the wire and the thickened section follows the central vein. Remove the veiner.

♣ Starting at the edge of the pattern left by the veiner on the paste closest to the wire, on the same side of the leaf as you use your tools, use a craft knife to flick the excess paste away from the leaf shape you are creating. This flicking action gives you a roughly serrated edge which is very realistic. The tip of the leaf should be cut to an elongated, sharp point. Continue the serration by turning the leaf over once the tip is reached.

♣ Soften the edge of the leaf with a dog bone tool on a foam pad. Set the leaves over different shapes to get realistic shapes. When the leaves are dry enough to hold their shape but not brittle, dust them. The smaller leaves are a lighter, sharper green than the larger leaves. The large leaves also tend to have quite a bit of browning on the edges and some insect damage. Arrange the leaves so there are sections of them that do not have anything immediately behind them. Heat a scriber in the flame of a cigarette lighter until it is red hot, then burn small holes into the leaf. Glaze the leaf with a ½-glaze.

PASTILLAGE

I have used pastillage fairly simply in this book to make cards and the small oval box.

It is a medium which appeals strongly to architects and engineers, as it can be used to construct scale models of buildings and furnishings. At the Salons Culinaire it is possible to see some masters at work in this medium, which can also be used to emulate very fine porcelain and china.

PASTILLAGE

1 quantity royal icing (see page 139)
1½ teaspoons gum tragacanth
220–250 g (7–8 oz) icing sugar, carefully sifted

♣ Sieve the gum tragacanth and 60 g (2 oz) of the icing sugar together. Stir into the royal icing. Sieve the remainder of the icing sugar on to a work surface. Gather the royal icing and gum tragacanth mixture into a ball and place on the work surface on a little of the icing sugar. Gently but swiftly knead in the icing sugar until the paste becomes pliable.

♣ Wrap the pastillage in cling film, then place it in a plastic bag. Store in an airtight container.

♣ Always keep the paste you are working with covered unless you are actually rolling or cutting it out! Use a minimum of icing sugar to roll it out on. Use a pizza wheel for a clean cut.

OVAL BOX

♣ Make the pastillage, roll out and cut the pieces as on page 141.

♣ Roll out the two ovals, cut them out and allow them to dry. The base of the box should be quite thick to lend weight and balance to the piece. The larger oval should be a little finer, but not translucent. It makes it easier

> Do not force the lid on to the box. If you have a slight protrusion somewhere, remove it with a little judicious sanding.

if you have a reasonable edge to attach the side to; but if the top of the lid is too thick it will make the box top-heavy. Place the drying ovals on a completely flat, smooth surface dusted lightly with cornflour. Keep turning the pieces over.

♣ Smooth the cut edges gently with an emery board if there are tiny rough patches on the ovals.

♣ Cut cardboard templates of the sides of the box and lid. Join the ends together to form an oval hoop using double-sided tape. They will support the sides and lid while the paste is drying.

♣ Cut out the piece of pastillage for the side of the box. Place it around the oval base and cut away any excess of paste. The two ends should only just overlap. Moisten the edge with a little gum glue and press together to get a neat join. If your pressure has stretched the paste, cut off any protruding. Join the sides of the box and lid to their oval with a fine line of royal icing.

♣ Seal the sides tightly to the lid and base. Place the cardboard form in to support the sides. Once they are dry, fill any gaps with a spot of royal icing. Smooth off carefully and allow to dry. Smooth the edges of the lid and box sides.

♣ Cut out the inner lining of the base of the box, attaching it so it protrudes above the side, making sure it is all level. The ends of the damp pastillage may be stuck together with egg white, but attach to the side with royal icing.

♣ When it is all dry, see that the lid fits on to the base of the box.

♣ Decorate the edges of the lid with gold food colouring mixed with oil or gin or vodka.

♣ Make the violas and their leaves and attach to the lid.

Passion Flower Cake

20 cm (8 inch) oval cake
36 cm (14 inch) oval cake
board
White sugarpaste
5 mm ($\frac{1}{4}$ inch) violet
ribbon to decorate
Violet picot-edged
ribbon for board edge
1 small celpick

•

FOR THE SPRAY
2 or 3 passion flowers
1 bud
5 or 7 passion flower
leaves
1 butterfly
Nile green tape

•

BUTTERFLY

Paste
White pastillage or
flowerpaste (see pages
102 and 138)

•

Cutter
Butterfly cutter/mould of
your choice

•

Colours
Black paste colour, violet
paste colour, sky blue
iridescent colour, lilac
iridescent colour, white
folk paint

The passion flower I have produced is a hybrid *P. mollissima*, modified to suit the cake. If some expert thinks a new plant has been discovered – it has, but only in my imagination!

♣ Cover the cake and board with white sugarpaste.
♣ When the sugarpaste is dry, attach the cake to the board. Fasten the violet ribbon around the base of the cake, finishing the join with a tiny bow. Edge the board with the picot-edged ribbon the same colour as that around the base of the cake. If liked, pipe a fine snailtrail around the lower edge.
♣ Tape the flowers and leaves into a natural looking spray.
♣ Insert the small celpick in to the end of the cake about half way down. Arrange the flowers to curve gracefully over the end of the cake towards the centre. Fasten the decorated butterfly to the surface of the cake at the front with a little royal icing. If you prefer, bind in a wired butterfly to hover over the spray.

BUTTERFLY
♣ Roll out the pastillage or paste very finely over the vein on a grooved board or using a grooved rolling pin. Very lightly dust the paste with cornflour.
♣ Cut out the shape, make sure the edges are not rough and set to dry in a shallow v-shape of kitchen foil or cardboard. If you wish you may add some fine miniature stamens to make the

feelers although this makes the butterfly rather heavy.
♣ Paint the whole butterfly with a deep wash of violet. When this is dry, dust the upper wing with the lilac iridescent colour and the lower one with the iridescent sky blue. Paint on the white dots in folk paint then paint in the black detail.

PASSION FLOWER

Paste
White, mid green, pale green

•

Cutters
Azalea (499), daphne (466), bittersweet leaf (577, 578)

•

Veiners
Fine orchid, bittersweet leaf

•

Stamens
Large white hammerseed

•

Wire
30-gauge white, 26-gauge white, 26-gauge green, 22-gauge

•

Tape
Nile green

•

Thread
120-gauge

•

Dusts
Dark green mixture, lime green, cornflower blue, plum, white, black, lemon yellow

♣ Make small hooks in three 30-gauge wires. Cover the hooks with small pieces of pale green paste. Tape these together and tilt the heads outwards and down. Below the pistil, bind on five stamens that have been tinted with lemon yellow dust.

♣ Place a cocktail stick alongside your finger then bind the thread around them thirty times. Break off the thread, fold it into a figure of eight and then thread a 30-gauge wire through the two loops. Cut through the loops and neaten the top. Dip the threads in egg white, blot off the excess egg white, curve the threads slightly using a pair of fine-nosed tweezers. Dust with the plum and cornflower blue, leaving the threads pale near the base and dusting on a light stripe of black about midway down the threads. Fasten this to the point where the stamens are attached to the stem of the passion flower.

♣ To make the calyx, roll out a piece of white paste, leaving a fairly long and slender throat. Use the azalea cutter to cut out the shape. Leaving the piece in place on your board, gently elongate the sepals by rolling a medium celstick along them. Broaden them slightly by rolling a cocktail stick or small celstick from the central line outwards. Open the throat fairly deeply using a medium celstick. Vein each sepal using the veining tool after veining it with the fine orchid petal veiner.

♣ Roll out another piece of white paste, cut out another azalea shape, this time without a throat. Treat it the same way as the sepals. Moisten the centre of the petals and attach firmly to the sepals.

♣ Use a celstick to re-open the throat. Use a pair of square tweezers to pinch a ridge around the centre of the flower. Pinch it irregularly around the ridge to make little nodules protruding from the ridge. Moisten the stem holding the pistil, stamen and filaments and gently pull this into the throat. Dust the petals with the cornflower blue and plum dust, the sepals a little less, and dust some lime green on to the back of the sepals.

♣ At the base of the pedicel, attach a green bract cut out freehand from some mid green paste. Mark veins on this before pinching on to the base of the flower.

♣ To make the tendril, bind a piece of 26-gauge wire around a celstick and attach to the plant at a junction of a leaf.

♣ The leaves are cut out from pale green paste using a bittersweet leaf cutter. The two side leaves are increased in size by rolling the paste larger. Vein the leaves using the bittersweet veiners. The two side leaves will need to be veined with the small veiner as the veins on the actual leaf veiner will be too small to reach the edge of the enlarged side leaves. Using a dresden tool serrate the edge of the leaves.

♣ Dust down the centre of the leaves with some of the dark green dust, then glaze with a ½-glaze. The leaves are arranged alternately on the plant.

♣ Make a slender bud, groove with a five-wire cage, add a bract at the base and add to the arrangement.

VICTORIAN DÉCOUPAGE
In Pastillage or Flowerpaste

♣ This is a very simple technique. First, find a design you like and trace it. Each design is 'lifted' by repeating the pieces that appear closest to you over and over again until you have a two-dimensional effect. The final layers do not have a great deal of pieces to them. Turn the tracing over and using a 2B pencil go over the design again on the underside of the paper. Repeat this process for each layer in the design.

♣ Roll out flowerpaste or pastillage and, while it is still damp, 'iron' the design on to the paste by using a smoother flat against the tracing paper, pressing down on the tracing and paste in broad circular movements. Remove the tracing. Place the piece of paste on a cutting board and very carefully cut out the design, removing any pieces of background that may also be incorporated within the design. Set the pieces aside to dry by placing them on a lightly cornfloured flat board. Turn them over at regular intervals so they dry evenly and flat.

♣ Turn the design face down on to a foam pad and, using a dresden tool, dog bone or celstick, raise the section that needs lifting by stretching the paste, applying some pressure and stroking the area being worked on.

♣ Transfer the background design on to the cake, plaque or card and paint the detail on to the pieces which make up the finished design. You can use moistened petal dust, folk paint, thinned down paste colour or cocoa butter and petal dust mixed together. Each of these media gives a slightly different effect. Experiment and see which one or which combination you prefer. It is not necessary to paint in all the detail on each layer. The first few layers where there are very large areas covered by the next layer you need decorate only the section of the design which might be seen from the side.

♣ One of the secrets of this method is to roll the flowerpaste or pastillage until it is translucent. Use a No. 2 tube to cut out small discs of the paste and stick these on to the surface of the lower layers with a little royal icing. This 'lifts' the design. If working on découpage with paper, one separates the layers either with bath sealant or cut up 'sticky fixers'; these small discs of paste separate the sugar layers in the same way.

CHRISTENING
CAKE

24 × 16 cm (9½ × 6½
inch) ellipse cake
34 × 24 (13½ × 9½ inch)
ellipse cake board
White sugarpaste
Découpage pieces
White royal icing
No. 0 Bekenal tube
No. 2 Bekenal tube
Wilton flower pick

•

FOR THE SPRAY
3 double bounce bows
with medium tails
3 sprays of Chinese
jasmine (see page 35)
1 pink full rose
(all-in-one) (see page 44)
5 pink half roses
(all-in-one) (see page 45)
5 pink rosebuds
7 trails of birdsfoot ivy;
2 long, 2 medium and
3 short (see page 17)

A pretty christening cake with a beautiful flower spray and an old-fashioned crib design. Choose the colours for the découpage pieces to suit a baby boy or girl.

♣ Cover the cake and board with white sugarpaste. Cut a template from the cake tin used. Place the template on the board where the cake will be positioned, then remove the sugarpaste from this section. Crimp the board with a suitable crimper. Set aside to dry. Insert the flower pick into the front of the cake (on this occasion the cake is presented with one of the narrow ends facing forwards) about 1 cm (½ inch) from the board. Leave the rim of the flower pick standing proud of the icing by about 2.5 mm (⅛ inch). This makes it much easier for the person cutting the cake to see that it is there and thus remove it from the cake before the cake is cut into slices. Pipe a fine snailtrail around the cake where the cake joins the board.

♣ Wire up the spray and have it ready to insert into the flower pick once the cake top is completed.

♣ Paint the background on to the surface of the cake. Paint the detail on to the découpage pieces. Adjust the colours according to whether the baby is male or female. Stack them one on top of the other, separated by the small flowerpaste or pastillage discs cut with a No. 2 tube and a little royal icing. (The design templates are on page 142.)

♣ Push the spray into the flowerpick and arrange the flowers attractively.

20 cm (8 inch)
heart-shaped cake
30 cm (12 inch)
heart-shaped cake board
Pale pink sugarpaste
Pink picot-edged ribbon
Pink 5 mm ($\frac{1}{4}$ inch)
ribbon to match
2 pale grey elephants
18-gauge wire
Flower-covered heart
Medium celpick
A little pink royal icing

•

FOR THE SPRAYS
2 long and two medium
trails of birdsfoot ivy (see
page 17)
25 small pink rosebuds
(see page 45)
30 small pink half-roses
50 pale blue flowers
30 pale blue buds
90 small leaves, wired
into threes

Hearts and Flowers

ENGAGEMENT CAKE

The flower sprays at the front of this heart–shaped cake are intended to look like the water at the prow of a boat, washing back to the ivy leaves below the two amorous elephants.

♣ Cover the cake and board with pale pink sugarpaste. Crimp the edge of the board with a suitable crimper. Leave to dry.

♣ Once the sugarpaste has set, place the cake on the board. Attach the pale pink ribbon around the base of the cake, covering the join with a tiny bow. Stick the picot ribbon to the board, making sure the join is in the identation at the back.

♣ Make two elephants, aiming the trunks in opposite directions to reach towards one another. One should have a bow tie and be fractionally larger than the other, which has a pretty bow above one ear.

♣ Take a full length piece of 18-gauge wire, bend it in half sharply and then curve it downwards away from the bend. Starting near the bend, bind in the blue flowers, leaves, rosebuds and roses. The flowers should point towards the bend from both directions. Tape the wire together firmly at the base and reshape the heart you have thus formed. Tape this on to another shorter, double length of 18-gauge wire. This will go into the celpick towards the back on the left hand side of the cake.

♣ Stick the elephants in place in front of the flower-covered heart, using a little pink royal icing.

♣ Wire up two identical sprays starting with a long and a medium trail of ivy leaves. Fasten the sprays firmly together, lifting the flowers at the front to hide the join. Curve the sprays backwards and attach to the front of the board against the cake with a little royal icing. Fill in any gaps with loose flowers or leaves.

Elephants: Take a piece of paste. Divide it into a sausage and five balls: one large ball, one approximately a third its size, two balls half the size of the smaller of these two balls. Divide one of the latter in half. Roll the larger ball into a slightly conical shape (it is more round than cone shaped, but you want it slightly narrower at the top). Gently pinch in a ridge down the back. Use two fingers on either side of the centre line opposite the ridge to mark the positions for the legs. Make a small dent in the top of the ball/cone for the bottom of the head to fit into.

♣ Make a small hole at the back of the body, on the ridge. The

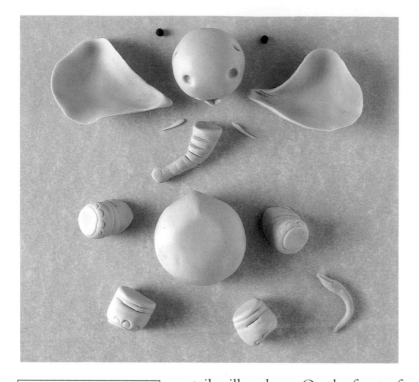

The elephants are quite simple to make. They can be made from any paste you enjoy working with – for example half flowerpaste and half sugarpaste, pastillage, Mexican paste and so on.

Wait until the elephants are in place on the cake to add the tails – they are very vulnerable to breakage. Make them out of the same colour pale grey paste as the elephants, form a thickened tip, with a slender piece to go into the body. Using a pair of fine scissors, mark the thickened tip of the tail into hairs.

tail will go here. On the front of the body use a piping tube or celstick to indent a belly button.

❧ Roll the smaller piece of paste into a ball. Make two fairly deep holes high up on the side of the head. Two pieces of paste from the ears will fill them and thus give you a firmer join. Mark an indentation where the trunk will go just above the mouth which is made by pushing a dresden tool into the paste, curved side down. Move it from side to side to widen the hole, and then press down sharply to open the mouth. Pinch the bottom lip to a slight point. Make two small holes for the tusks just above and to the side of the mouth. Make two shallow depressions for the eyes.

❧ Turn the medium ball into the trunk, shaping the tip into two points, with two little holes for the nostrils. Mark lines on the trunk, pinch the paste between the lines into ridges and concertina it slightly with a little pressure. Set it in a curve to dry.

❧ Make the legs by cutting a roll

of paste into four pieces. Two of the pieces should be slightly larger than the other two. These will be the back legs. Roll neatly, crease lines into them with the back of a knife and concertina slightly. Stick small circles of pink paste on to the pads of the feet – I used the back of a piping tube to mark in the toes, part on and part off the pink pads.

❧ Using a little gum glue or egg white, stick the back legs in place against the body (I assembled them on small yoghurt pot lids). When these are set, add the front legs. Support with small pieces of foam until they have set.

❧ Fill the two depressions for the eyes with a little white paste. Paint eyes and eyelashes on to the paste with black paste colour. Attach the trunk to the head with a little gum glue and support on dimpled foam until it has set. Roll the two small balls of paste into teardrops and shape into the ears, softening the edges with a dog bone tool or celstick. Dust the inside of the ears pink. Insert the points of the ears into the holes at the side of the head (these have been moistened with a little gum glue). Press the paste firmly into the holes, arrange the ears. They must still be soft when the heads are attached to the bodies.

❧ Stick the head to the body with a little royal icing, being careful not to bump the trunk, and arranging the ears to come slightly between the body and the head, curving over the shoulders like a shawl. When this is dry, add the tusks. Colour the inside of the mouth with pinky/red dust, and the tip of the trunk with a little pale pink.

Enamelled Easter Egg

The pearly sheen of this elegant egg makes it instantly appealing. I based the idea on cloisonné work, in which enamels were used on gold or brass.

♣ Make the Easter egg. (If you don't want such a large egg, the design can be reduced on a photocopier or by the square method). While still in the two halves, transfer the design on to the egg. Be careful not to press on to the pastillage too heavily or it will snap.

♣ Fill it with sweets or cellophane-wrapped pieces of simnel cake. Stick the back and front together carefully. Dust with the South African bridal satin.

♣ Pipe the royal icing over the design and allow to dry. Pipe the three components that will make the finial, then allow to dry. Paint the royal icing lines and finial pieces gold with the moistened gold food colouring. Stick the three pieces together to form the finial. Allow to dry. Paint any white royal icing that may show with the gold colour.

♣ Mix the pearl dusts or hi-liters into the piping gel and carefully fill in the design.

♣ Attach the pastillage egg to the stand and support it carefully while the royal icing dries. Attach the finial to the top of the egg with royal icing.

ENAMELWORK

Find a design you like – it can be as simple or complicated as you wish to make it. Transfer the design to a piece of pastillage. Pipe the outlines with royal icing and a No. 0 Bekenal tube. Once the royal icing has set, very carefully paint the lines with gold colouring which has been moistened either with a clear spirit such as gin, or with cooking oil. Mix small quantities of the pearl dust or Hi-liters with clear piping gel and fill in the sections of the design with this enamel-like gel. You can use very small piping bags with a tiny hole cut from the tip; this does give you good control of where the 'enamel' is to go, but is fairly wasteful. Make several items at once so you can use all the colour you have mixed. If you don't want to use a piping bag you can use a tiny spoon and a paint brush to add the colour. In real cloisonné, the enamel comes right up to the top of the threads; with this sugar interpretation I leave the lines a little proud.

♣ Supporting the eggs so they don't roll over on to their decorated sides can be a problem. The piping gel takes a long time to set and is very sticky. Support the egg on an egg-crafting ostrich egg stand or use a chocolate mould which has the base of the egg flattened.

DECORATIVE TOUCHES

SUGARPASTE

To the uninitiated this seems to be
a very easy way to achieve a good
covering on a cake – it is deceptive.
Anyone can very easily cover a
cake, but achieving a *good*
covering is a very different matter.
That takes a great deal of skill.
I have used it to create a very
simple cake, but with the frills,
flounces, broiderie anglaise and so
on, it has many uses.

A Mother's Day Gift

30 cm (12 inch) teardrop
cake, marzipaned
36 cm (14 inch) oval cake
board
White sugarpaste
2 m (2 yds) hot pink
3 mm (⅛ inch) Offray
ribbon
4 flounces made with
Garrett frill cutter
Royal icing

•

FOR THE LEAVES
heart-shaped cutters
(327, 328)
Stephanotis cutter (568)

•

FOR THE FLOWERS
6 cyclamen buds, 25
leaves, 15 flowers
1 celpot

Just the right present for a beloved mother, this cake could be either sponge or fruit. It combines being good to eat and good to look at with the traditional gift of flowers.

❧ Cover the cake and board with white sugarpaste. Cut a template from the cake tin used. Place the template on the board where the cake will be positioned, then remove the sugarpaste from this section. Finish off the board by crimping the edges. Leave to set.

❧ When the sugarpaste has set, place the cake on the board. Cut a long strip of greaseproof paper to the circumference of the cake, plus 2.5 cm (1 inch). Cut the paper the same depth as the coated cake. Remove the paper from the cake. Join it together, overlapping the cut edges by 1 cm (½ inch) either side.

❧ Decide on the shape the decoration should take and cut the greaseproof paper accordingly. This is your template. Place the template over the cake again and mark the design on the cake with a scriber.

❧ Pipe a fine snailtrail of sugarpaste softened with a liqueur around the base of the cake to seal it. Decorate the base of the cake with a narrow band of ribbon which tones with the flower colouring. Finish off the join with a tiny ribbon bow.

❧ To make the flounces, knead equal amounts of sugarpaste and flowerpaste together. Roll out thinly and cut out pieces with a 13 cm (5 inch) Garrett frill cutter. Roll the edges of the circles with the small celstick or a cocktail stick to make a flounce. Stick the flounce in position, decorating the upper edge as shown.

❧ For the side decoration, paint the curving stems of the buds and flowers on to the cake with a fine brush.

❧ Make the leaves by cutting out small hearts, frill the edge with a dresden tool. Paint a little light colour on to the leaf to represent the variegation.

DECORATIVE TOUCHES

116

Using a small stephanotis cutter, roll out the pink paste thinly. Cut out a shape, gently soften the centre of each petal with a cocktail stick without broadening them too much. Insert a cocktail stick into the centre, fold the petals back towards the tip, pinching firmly. Flatten them gently. Dust the centre of the flower with same dust you used for the flowers, tip the centre with white.

Stick the flowers and leaves on to the surface of the cake with a little egg white.

Make the cyclamen flowers, buds and leaves, then arrange them in the celpot. I wanted my flowers to look as though they were growing from the board so I softened some sugarpaste with liqueur, stuck the celpot in place after I had made a mossy area around the celpot by pushing softened coloured paste through a cheap nylon sieve.

If you want to you may add a greeting and name to the surface of the cake, but I do not like writing on the cake itself. I prefer to write on a separate sugar scroll in case I mess up many hours of hard work!

FRILLS AND FLOUNCES

There is some confusion over what makes a Garrett frill and what makes a Garrett flounce.

Very few people actually do the Garrett frill. This is carried out by cutting out a circle of sugarpaste or half sugarpaste/half flowerpaste with a Garrett frill cutter. Cut the frill apart in one place and slightly straighten it out. Using a cocktail stick, press lines into the scallops. You will need to press about twelve to fifteen lines into each little scallop. This stretches the paste and makes it lift, but on this occasion it looks a bit like pleated organza.

You can use this idea to make the Garrett frill shells which I have used on the Waterlily christening cake (see page 121). Mark lines from one end of the scallop to the centre point of the scallop and repeat the same movement from the other end. This gives you a peak above the scallop. Now press the stick into the paste in lines moving from one end of the scallop to the other until the whole thing is marked. Gently lift up the stretched paste to form a little shell.

The Garrett flounce is what most people incorrectly call the Garrett frill. To make a Garrett flounce, roll a cocktail stick, celstick or anything similar firmly along the edge of the shape cut out with the Garrett frill cutter, cut through and attach to the cake. This gives a lovely softly flounced decoration.

117

Paste
*Pink, red, mauve,
white – your choice;
dark green and mid green
– holly/ivy green*

•

Cutters
*Bridal gladiolus large
petal (467), smallest
calyx (R13), variegator
(440) heart-shaped (333,
332)*

•

Veiners
*Poppy petal, cyclamen
leaf or large violet leaf*

•

Wire
24-gauge, 28-gauge

•

Tape
White

•

Dusts
*Pale green and white
mixture, moss and apple
green mixture, burgundy
mixture (2 parts plum,
1 part red, 1 part
cornflower blue, 1 part
nutkin brown and $\frac{1}{4}$ part
black – it is worth mixing
this in large quantities as
it is a very useful colour),
white dust or white
paste colour*

CYCLAMEN

♣ For the flowers, cut the wires to half-length or taller. For each stem bind a 24-gauge wire with white tape. The stems should be fine at the junctions of the flowers, but thick and fleshy at ground level. To do this, gradually thicken the wire from one end. The first taping should be for about 2.5 cm (1 inch), then break tape off. Then start at the same point as before and tape for 5 cm (2 inch), then break off. The next layer should be taped from the same starting point to 7.5 cm (3 inch) etc. Once you get to the top, give the wire a final covering from top to bottom. After you have thickened the wires, dust them with the moss and apple green mixture and burgundy mixture dusts.

♣ Take a small ball of paste of your chosen colour for the flower petals. Make a small hook at the fine end of a taped wire. Moisten the hook and insert into the small ball of paste, fastening it on securely. With the small end of a dog bone tool, cup the ball of paste so you have a fairly deep depression with a relatively fine edge. Do not make the edge too fine or it will cut through the petals when you attach them.

♣ Cut out a calyx from thinly rolled-out mid green paste. Place on a piece of kitchen paper and carefully dust the edges with the burgundy dust. Then, using the white dust, lighten the extreme edge of the calyx. Place, coloured edge down, on a foam pad and firmly mark down the centre of each sepal with a veiner. Cut a slit into the calyx and wrap it around the flower cup, rejoining the cut section. Allow to dry for

24 hours. Dust the flower stem before the petals are stuck in place.

♣ Roll out the paste fairly thinly for the petals. Cut out five petals per flower (have a few extra to allow for mistakes). With the broader end facing you, gently broaden each petal at the widest part, leaving the base of the petal unchanged. Elongate the petals slightly by rolling off the tip of each petal fairly firmly. Make sure the five petals match one another. Now vein the petals, having the narrow part of each petal at the base of the veiner. Squeeze firmly. Gently roll a cocktail stick around the upper edge of each petal to flute it gently. Using the cocktail stick, gently shape the petals by rolling one side of each petal inwards.

♣ Insert the thickened end of the flower stem into a block of oasis or something similar (you need to be able to turn the flower in this upright position). Moisten the inner edge of the cup with a little egg white taken just over the edge to the outside of the cup. Do not moisten too much of the outside of the cup.

♣ Gently lift a petal, put the base of the petal inside the cup and drape it over the cup edge. Align the petals so that the petal joins match the tips of the sepals. Gently pinch the petal in place, gently pulling upwards as you do so. This gives a very tight bond to the cup and allows a fraction of the petal to join to itself. Gently press a celstick or skewer on to this exposed piece of petal so that the edges of the petal at the sepal joins are slightly higher than the centre of the petal. Repeat this process five times. The petals should be next to one another, not overlapping at all. Gently twist and tweak the petals

to get a realistic shaping. There should be one spot where there is a slight gap between two petals. This is where the stem will fit once the stem is curved over into position. Dry in the upright position.

♣ When the petals are firmly in place but not yet brittle, dust the centre of the flower with the burgundy mixture. Now dust a streak of darker toning colour part-way up the centre of each petal. Using white paste colour or moistened white dust, very carefully paint the lifted edges of the petal where it is attached to the cup.

♣ To arrange the flowers, curve the stems by grasping them immediately behind the calyx using a very small, pointed pair of pliers or a pair of strong tweezers. Hold the stem very firmly with the tool and with your other hand, very gently but firmly push the stem upwards, aiming for the slight gap between the petals.

♣ *Bud*: Cut 24-gauge wires into thirds and tape as for the flowers, but not so thickly. To make a bud, roll a piece of paste of your chosen colour into a narrow carrot shape. Insert a moistened, hooked, tape-thickened wire into the broad base. Fasten firmly with your fingers, cutting the paste off neatly at the junction.

♣ Make a cage by fastening five 28-gauge wires together with a piece of tape. Open the cage slightly, spreading the wires evenly. Insert the pointed end of the bud into the cage and gently close the cage around the piece of paste, making sure that the wires

For more realism, have some slightly drooping flowers as well. Use the steam from a saucepan of boiling water with a slanted lid or a kettle without an automatic switch. Then very quickly flash *all* the buds, flowers and leaves with a little steam to set the dust, so that the drooping flowers do not look different from the others.

Cyclamen flowers look far better as a growing plant, rather than arranged into a spray. Unless you actually make a plant pot for the plant to fit into, you can arrange the stems into a celpot, which may be attached either to the cake or to the board of the cake where the flowers are to be used. Be very careful to hide the pot and the holding material with your leaves.

The buds and flowers are taller than the leaves. Some buds look interesting if you spiral the stem. To do this, grasp the stem very firmly with a pair of fine-nosed pliers or tweezers and gently spiral the stem a couple of times before taking it back in the direction that the bud points to.

are evenly distributed. Holding the taped end in one hand and the gathered wires in the other, gently pull your hands apart. Holding the cage closed tightly at the base, gently pinch each protruding piece of paste until it is very fine. At this stage it looks rather strange with each petal standing out at right angles from the wire. Gently remove the cage.

♣ Form the fingers and thumb of your left hand (if you are right-handed) into a circle and insert the bud into the centre. Very gently rotate the wire you are holding in your right hand away from yourself. Gradually tighten the circle until the petals are tightly spiralled. You can make some of the buds partly unfurled.

♣ Cut out, dust and vein a calyx as for the flower (see page 118). Moisten the back of the bud with egg white and pull the wire through the calyx. This is quite a tricky operation with the wire having been thickened. Dust the edges of the petals gently with a slightly deeper colour than that of the paste used. Buds are usually slightly darker than the flowers. Dust the white-taped wires with a mixture of the green and burgundy dusts.

♣ *Leaves*: Cut 24-gauge wires into quarters and tape as for the flowers, but not so thickly. Using a grooved board or rolling pin, roll out sufficient dark green paste for one leaf. Using a heart-shaped cutter or the leaf veiner as a template, cut out the leaf. Insert the narrow end of a tape-thickened wire into the central vein. Press the leaf firmly on to the veiner. With the tip of a dresden tool, pull out small

sections of paste from the edge of the leaf to form serrations. Place the leaf on a foam pad and with a dog bone tool, very carefully soften the edge of the leaf. Using the greeny white dust, a suitable liquid and a very fine brush, paint pale veins on the leaf. Set aside to dry in an interesting shape.

♣ When firm but not brittle, roll out more paste and cut out a shape with the variegator. If it is a small leaf, leave it that size; as the leaves increase in size, roll out the variegator cutter pieces to a suitable size. Attach the variegator shape to the centre of the leaf, positioning it just above the junction of the wire. Do not moisten the shape; use only the natural adhesive qualities of the freshly rolled out paste.

♣ Moisten some of the greeny white dust and with a coarse brush, stipple the colour over the junction of the variegator shape and the dark green leaf. Now carefully stipple a pattern of greeny white on to the leaf. With a large, flat brush, gently brush the mixture of moss and apple green on to the edge of the leaf up to the greeny white pattern. Dust the underside of the leaf heavily with the burgundy mixture, gently bringing it right to the edge of the leaf, so on the right side you get a hint of the burgundy colour at the edge. Do not dust it on to the edge from the front of the leaf, as that makes the burgundy edge too harsh.

♣ Remove the variegator shape and you will have a beautifully stencilled design on the leaf. Dust the white stem with both the green and the burgundy dust.

20 cm (8 inch) oval cake
30 cm (12 inch) oval cake
board
Pale blue sugarpaste
Tiny butterfly/dragonfly
cutter/veiner
White Mexican paste or
half sugarpaste and half
flowerpaste (page 138)
Garrett frill cutter
Waterlily pram
5 mm (¼ inch) pale blue
ribbon
Blue picot-edged ribbon

•

FOR THE PRAM
Paste
White, mid green

•

Cutters
Circle (292), Cattleya
narrow side petals (325,
11 and 8), 2 heart-shaped
(330, 329)

•

Veiners
Finely veined orchid
petal, large nasturtium
leaf

•

Stamens
Lily

•

Wire
28-gauge white,
20-gauge

•

Tape
Nile green

•

Dust
Spectral lemon yellow,
cornflower blue, white,
dark green mixture

Waterlily Pram Cake

This unusual decoration was designed specifically for my new grandson's christening cake. Both the cake and decoration had to be pretty, special but fairly sturdy as the christening was held in Antigua!

♣ Cover the cake and board with pale blue sugarpaste. Crimp the edge of the board with a suitable crimper. Leave to dry.
♣ Place the cake on the board. Fasten the pale blue ribbon around the base of the cake, finishing the join with a tiny bow. Neaten the edge of the board with picot-edged ribbon.
♣ Make a template the height and circumference of the cake, mark into shallow scallops. Mark on to the cake. About 8 mm (⅓ inch) above this line, mark another line. Roll out a little paste, cut out the tiny dragonflies and butterflies. Use to decorate the upper marked line.
♣ Roll and cut out the correct number of shapes for the Garrett frill. Using a cocktail stick, press into each scallop forming the Garrett frill shells. Stick the upper edge of the frill to the cake with a little clear alcohol.
♣ Place the pram on the cake at an attractive angle.

If you are not putting a baby in the pram, you will need stamens. Working with the larger bunch of stamens, tape a layer of the small petals around the stamens. This looks best if you start with three petals evenly distributed and then tape in the next three just behind and between the first layer. Repeat this same process with six medium petals, and then with twelve large petals. Now tape in the three large petals which have been dusted green and glazed. These petals form the calyx and should be evenly distributed around the flower.

Repeat the same process around the smaller bunch of stamens, only this time use twice the number of medium petals to form the outer petal layers, backing the petals with the calyx made of three medium petals dusted green and glazed.

❧ Roll out mid green paste on a Mexican hat board using a medium sized hole for the centre (the paste must not be too thin). Vein the leaf with the nasturtium leaf veiner. Smooth the edge with a dog bone tool. Cut a narrow, deep V into the centre of the leaf.

❧ Make a small circle at the end of the 20-gauge wire, bend it sideways and cover the wire using the green tape. Heat the circle using a cigarette lighter. When it is red hot, press the circle into the central knob in the middle of the leaf. Repeat this for all four leaves. Dust the centre of the leaf with dark green mixture and glaze with $\frac{3}{4}$ glaze.

❧ Roll out the white paste using a grooved board or pin. Roll out the paste near what will be the tip of the petal, cut out the petal, soften the edge and insert a moistened 28-gauge white wire into the central vein. Vein the petal with the orchid veiner. Soften the edge with the dog bone tool. Using the veining tool, stroke strongly down the centre of the leaf from the tip to the base, being careful not to cut through the paste or expose the wire. Set into a curve to dry.

❧ Make twelve small petals, twenty-one medium petals and fifteen large petals. Dust the petals lightly with a mixture of cornflower blue and white petal dust. Three each of the large and medium petals are dusted with dark green on the underside of the curve. Glaze these petals with a $\frac{1}{2}$-glaze. Dust the lily stamens with the lemon yellow dust. Tape two bunches on to 20-gauge wire. One bunch should be larger than the other.

❧ Stamens should be added at this point if required, see Tip box (left).

❧ Tape two pairs of leaves together. The wire should be bent to a right angle about 1 cm ($\frac{1}{2}$ inch) from where they are attached to the wheel. Bend both pairs of taped together leaves at another right angle and tape all four wires into a single stem which emerges from the centre point between the four leaf wheels.

❧ The leaves should be about 4–5 cm ($1\frac{1}{2}$–2 inch) apart, and the two pairs should be about 5 cm (2 inch) apart. Divide the four wires into two and tape them this way. About 1 cm ($\frac{1}{2}$ inch) above the wheels, bend the wires forward and curve them gently upwards. Trim off some of the 28-gauge wires from behind the smaller waterlily. Tape to a 20-gauge wire. Tape over this several times to get a smooth stem. Bend this wire into a graceful curve. Tape this to the stem formed below the larger waterlily, thinning out some of the wires. The upper waterlily should form the pram hood. Divide the wires below the larger waterlily into two. Tape them. Now tape them to the wires curving from the wheels. Rest the waterlily on the wheels, and curve the two bunches of wires into graceful curves to make the handles. Support the pram on its side while you make sure the wheels below the hood are attached firmly to the central stalk of the waterlily. Spread the petals attractively.

❧ Using the two heart-shaped cutters, make a pillow. Roll out a small piece of white paste, cut

it out with the larger heart–shaped cutter. Frill the edge with a cocktail stick. The paste for the smaller heart should be quite thick. Cut out the shape and soften the edges of the heart with your fingers. Moisten the underside of the heart and fasten it to the centre of the frilled heart.

❧ Make a tiny baby using a piece of paste in a suitable colour. Roll into a teardrop. With the side of your finger, make a small round piece at the top. Taper the rest of the piece to a point. Dust the colour of the hair to that chosen.

❧ Place the pillow in the waterlily directly below the hood. Moisten the underside of the baby slightly and stick it to the pillow. Roll out a fine piece of white paste, emboss or decorate it as you wish and, cutting it into a blanket shape, fold back one end and then tuck it over the baby. Dust lightly.

ROYAL ICING

I felt I had to include some royal icing techniques in this book to make it complete. Unfortunately it is not a medium that I am comfortable with. It needs discipline and a steady hand – I have neither. Some people find extension work and piping very soothing – how different they are from me. I studied Ronnie Rock's magnificent cake at the National Bakery School for hour upon hour when I was studying there. I knew I could never achieve his standard of perfection.

Damask Rose Cake

The decoration on this beautiful cake combines several techniques. The cake is adorned with a pleated drape, intricate filet crochet extension work and a damask rose.

30 cm (12 inch) teardrop cake
36 cm (14 inch) oval cake board
Pale green sugarpaste
175 g (6 oz) pale peach Mexican paste (see page 138)
Pale peach royal icing
No. 00 Bekenal tube
Heavy duty kitchen foil
Pale peach picot-edged ribbon for board edge
Small oblongs of 5 mm ($\frac{1}{4}$ inch) perspex
South African Hi-Liter or pearl dusts

•

FOR THE SPRAY
1 damask rose
1 damask rosebud
Damask rose leaves

♣ Cover the cake and board with the pale green sugarpaste. Crimp the edge of the board with a suitable crimper. Cut a template from the cake tin used. Place the template on the board where the cake will be positioned, then remove the sugarpaste from this section. Leave to dry.

PLEATED DRAPE

♣ Colour the Mexican paste a pale peach. This is more than you will need, but it is better to have too much as it would be difficult to match up the same colour later.
♣ Measure the circumference of the cake. Add on approximately 10 cm (4 inch) to be absolutely sure you will have a long enough piece of paste.
♣ Take a piece of kitchen foil three times the length of the circumference of the cake plus a little extra. Fold it into three and pleat it firmly along the length of the foil. Gently spread the pleats out a little.
♣ Roll out the piece of Mexican paste at least 12 cm ($4\frac{1}{4}$ inch) wide, and the length of the circumference of the cake plus the 10 cm (4 inch). Mexican paste is very flexible, but because of this flexibility it takes a good amount of strength to roll it out very finely, particularly when such a length is required. It is easier to

use a pasta maker to roll out the paste. Roughly roll out the paste using a rolling pin and then feed it through the pasta maker several times, increasing the roller pressure each time until the paste is as thin as possible. (It is far easier to do this with another pair of hands to help support the paste.)
♣ Lift the paste and lay it along the pleated foil. See that it is lying smoothly along the pleats. Gently concertina the pleats, stroking up and down the paste as you do so, so that it lies neatly in the grooves. When you have the pleats folded to your satisfaction, use a pizza wheel to cut away the paste you do not need.
♣ At the front of the cake, gather the pleated paste together firmly, moistening it slightly. Moisten the upper edge of the pleat which is to be attached to the upper surface of the cake; this is a gradual process. Once again it is much easier having someone to hold up the foil for you, supporting the paste while you are sticking it in place. Drape the pleated paste all the way around the cake allowing the pleating to open gently at the back of the cake so the pleats fall softly open down to the board at the back. Moisten the other end of the

pleated drape when you reach the front again. Pinch together firmly, moisten slightly and fasten the end alongside the starting point, cutting any excess paste away. Lightly brush the pleated paste with a South African Hi-Liter or pearl colour dust to match the pale peach. This will highlight the material look of the drape. Allow to dry.

FILET CROCHET EXTENSION WORK

It is vital that the royal icing is free flowing and elastic for this work. It is advisable that the icing sugar used is the bridal icing which does not have any cornflour added to it – you can test your sugar to see if it is pure by dissolving a couple of teaspoons in a tumbler of cold water. If the water is cloudy the icing has had the cornflour added to it. Unfortunately most of the manufacturers are now adding cornflour to the icing as an anticaking device. This may not affect day to day icing too severely, but it is a great handicap when doing very fine competition or extension work.

✤ Add two drops of acetic acid to the icing to make it more elastic. Be very careful not to add too much colour. Test the flow of the icing and its elastic qualities by dropping some icing between your thumb and forefinger. If it does not break when you have quite a long loop the icing will hold as you use it.

✤ This work is most easily done if you have a tilting turntable. If not you will have to prop up the back of the cake. These two methods tilt the cake forwards so the icing will fall away from the surface of the cake. Keep changing the angle by moving the cake

slightly after a few strands have been piped in place.

✤ Pipe a long curving line of icing on to a plastic file cover or a piece of cellophane, allow to dry. The design is shown on page 143. Pipe a fine snailtrail around the base of the cake. Once this icing is dry, position a number of perspex oblongs, 5 mm (¼ inch) deep along the board. Lift the curved piece of icing and position it against the cake supporting it on the perspex. Attach either end to the cake using a tiny spot of icing.

✤ Tilt the cake towards you and, starting at the centre of the deepest drop of the extension lines, pipe the extension lines down on to the curved line of icing. Attach all the extension lines to the underside of the drape. Remember to go past the line on each occasion so you do not get bumps of icing forming on the support line. Use a very fine brush, very lightly moistened, to take off any untidy pieces of icing. Allow these lines

DAMASK ROSE CAKE

to dry. Now pipe the horizontal lines in place making neat squares. This is an extremely painstaking part of the work. Strengthen the base of the extension by adding short downstrokes between the extension lines in the lowest square. Finish off the edge of the crochet with a picot decoration.

♣ Draw out your design for the filet work on to a piece of squared paper. Calculate the position of the decoration you are using. Use the squared paper as a guide when counting the squares on the extension work. Pipe two short vertical lines into each square to form your pattern. When you have done this outline the design with a No. 00 tube.

♣ Finish the cake off by placing the damask rose over the join between the two ends of the pleated drape. The underside of the burgundy petals of the damask rose should be the same colour as the peach of the pleated drape and the royal icing of the extension work.

DAMASK ROSE

Paste
Ruby, chestnut, mid green

•

Cutters
Large rose petal (550, 551), calyx cutter (246)

•

Wire
20-gauge

•

Tape:
Nile green

•

Dust
Burgundy mixture (2 parts plum, 1 part cornflower blue; 1 part nutkin brown, 1 part red and $\frac{1}{4}$ part black)

♣ Make some large rose knobs (see page 21) using ruby paste and leave them to dry. Take a ball of ruby paste and a ball of chestnut paste half that size. Place the balls of paste on top of one another, with the ruby colour against the board. Roll out the paste finely and cut out the petals – ten petals with the 551 cutter and seven to ten with the 550 cutter.

♣ *Layer 1*: Soften the edge of one 551 petal, moisten most of the red side and wrap it firmly around the knob. Roll back the side edge. Before adding the next layer, dust the back of the petal with a mixture of champagne and peach dust. Do not get any on the red side of the petal.

♣ *Layer 2*: Soften the edges of three 551 petals. Cup the centre of each petal and roll back the upper top edges of the petals with a cocktail stick. Attach all three petals to the centre of the rose, the edges abutting one another, not crossing over one another. These petals should be slightly taller than the centre petal. Dust this layer of petals as for Layer 1.

♣ *Layers 3 and 4*: Repeat as for Layer 2. (The petals for layer 3 are cut with the 551 cutter. For layer 4 use the 550 cutter). The petals of each succeeding layer are placed over the joins of the previous one, and each layer is fractionally higher than the one before.

♣ *Layer 5*: The petals are cut using the 550 cutter. Soften the edges and cup the centre of each petal. Roll back the top edge of each petal and then the two sides. Arrange the petals on the rose one at a time, spacing them attractively. Dust the upper surface of the rose with burgundy dust.

♣ Do not make the calyx until the leaves and flowers have been made. When you are ready to assemble the spray, add the calyx whilst it is still moist. This prevents the calyx from breaking while you are wiring up the flowers.

♣ Make the rosebuds as described for the single petal rose (see page 45) and leaves as described earlier.

Brush Embroidered

MAGNOLIA CAKE

*33 cm (13 inch) scalloped
oval cake with a curve cut
into the front
40 cm (16 inch) oval cake
board
Champagne sugarpaste
White royal icing (see
page 139)
Piping gel
Various petal dusts
No. 0, 1, 2 Bekenal tubes*

•

FOR THE SPRAY
*1 magnolia bud
2 half-open magnolias
1 mature magnolia bound
together to form a branch
of flowers*

When making the magnolia spray, remember that it is unusual for magnolia leaves to be out at the same time as the flowers. Only the last few appear together.

♣ Cover the cake and board with champagne sugarpaste. Cut a template from the cake tin used, remembering to allow for the curve cut into the front of the cake. Place the template on the board where the cake will be positioned, then remove the sugarpaste from this section. Crimp the edge of the board with a crimper of your choice. Dust the crimped edge with a little pink petal dust. Allow to dry.

♣ Immediately after you have coated the cake with sugarpaste, transfer the brush embroidered design on to the surface. Allow the sugarpaste to set. Place the cake on the board, then pipe a fine snailtrail around the base.

♣ Paint in the design and dust it with petal dust – the same as used on the flowers.

♣ Place the magnolia spray on the board in the curved section of the cake.

BRUSH EMBROIDERY

♣ Choose a design, trace it with tracing paper and a 2B pencil. Turn the design over and repeat the tracing on the other side. Once again turn the design over, position it against the cake, and 'iron' the design on to the

icing with firm circular strokes using a smoother. Remove the tracing paper and the design should be clearly visible. Allow it to dry.

♣ For brush embroidery you will need freshly made royal icing which is at its full peak. For every four tablespoons of royal icing, add one teaspoon of clear piping gel. This slows down the drying time.

♣ Study the design, then start working on the sections that appear to be furthest away. If you only have a small section to cover, choose a 0 tube. A very large area will require something more substantial, particularly if it has to be built up because it is in the foreground.

♣ Outline the section with a suitable tube, being careful to pipe over the traced line. Pipe another line of icing immediately inside the first one. Using a damp, but not wet, paint brush, stroke the icing from the line to the central point of the design. Make sure the brush flows over the whole section.

♣ Brushing in a leaf one would usually be working towards the central line from both sides of the leaf. When painting in a long leaf

with parallel veining, keep your brush strokes flowing in this direction. Never brush across the vein lines of any petal, leaf or bud.

🍀 The petals, leaves etc. that appear closest in the picture need a greater amount of icing piped into them so that they are built up. Once the leaves have been brushed in you can remove some of the icing using a fine dry brush, leaving bare lines as your emphasis.

🍀 If you are working on a dark background, pale icing will give a lovely clear design that needs no other decoration. Similarly, if you have a white or cream background you can use a dark icing as your contrast. Some brush embroidery looks very good if you use the icing as you would embroidery thread. This is, however, very time consuming. I find I enjoy doing it most if I use self-colour icing to that of the background, and then very carefully and lightly petal dust the various colours after the icing has set.

It is also very important to bear shading in mind when working on a piece like this. Do not change the emphasis of light half way through a picture.

Paste
White, pale green, pale melon

•

Cutters
Magnolia (452–454), narrow side petals of cymbidium orchids (15, 18, 21 and 24)

•

Veiner
Gardenia

•

Wire
20-gauge, 26-gauge white and green, 32-gauge white

•

Tape
Brown, white

•

Dusts
Plum, pink, apple green, primrose yellow, lemon yellow, egg yellow, black, brown, nutkin brown, champagne, vine green

Magnolia

🍀 First make the centre. Insert the tip of a moistened brown covered wire into a roll of green paste two-thirds the length of the smallest petal. Starting at the top of the roll, use a fine pair of scissors to cut nicks into the paste. Gently curve them back. This forms the stigmatic cone.

🍀 The stamens are made by rolling small pieces of pale melon paste on to 32-gauge white wires. Make them into small banana shapes varying from 5–10 mm ($\frac{1}{4}$–$\frac{1}{2}$ inch) long. Dust the curved back tips of the stigmatic cone with champagne dust with a tiny touch of a combination of plum and pink at the very tips. Glaze the stigmatic cone with $\frac{3}{4}$-glaze. Set aside to dry. Dust the stamens with a combination of primrose, lemon yellow and egg yellow. Using the combination of plum and pink, dust the bases of the stamens. Bind the curving stamens around the base of the cone, starting with the shortest ones and gradually surrounding it with layers of these stamens.

🍀 Roll out the white paste on a grooved board – it should not be too thin. Make a minimum of three of each size tepal. There are usually between nine and 18. The tepals are arranged in two or more whorls with from three to six tepals in each layer.

🍀 *Layer 1*: This is the layer of tepals closest to the stamens, made using the medium sized cutter. Soften the edge of each tepal. Insert the tip of a moistened 26-gauge white wire into the thickened central vein. The further you can insert the wire into the vein the better. Use the largest black ball tool to cup the broad end of the tepal. The whole tepal should be curved. The inner layer of tepals have to be wired up curving around the stamens. To get the ideal shape, position a soft petal next to the wired centre, bend the wire to shape and leave to dry. Copy for the other tepals in this layer.

🍀 Using the mixture of plum and pink petal dust moistened to

The covering of the bud, called the perule, is usually rather hairy on the species of magnolia which flowers before the leaves appear. A greyish green dust gives a velvety look – moisten with steam and then roll in the dust.

On this type of magnolia the leaves really only appear after the flowers, but there is a period when the last few flowers on the tree are accompanied by some leaves. For sugarcraft purposes this is more appealing, as any flower is improved with greenery.

Magnolia flowers are very large and are best arranged draping over the cake from the board. Place any cake featuring large flowers on an extra large board.

a paste, paint very fine lines on the back of the tepals, radiating from the base to within 1 cm ($\frac{1}{2}$ inch) of the edge of the tepal. Once these lines are dry, lightly dust some more of these colours over the back of the petals. The lines should show through. The dusting is darkest at the base of the tepals. The inside of the tepals must be kept very white.

♣ *Layer 2*: For this layer, use the largest cutters in the set. Cut out three or six tepals, insert a moistened 26-gauge white wire as far up the vein as you can get it. Flatten out the upper part of the central vein with your fingers. Soften the edge of the tepal with a dog bone tool. Place the tepal on a foam pad with the inside of the tepal on the pad. Use a dog bone and the side of a celstick to curve back the upper curve of the tepal. Turn the tepal over and, using the largest black ball tool, cup the tepal firmly. Remember that the lowest part of the tepal will have to be curved around the base of the stamens, but it does have a larger curve at the broad end. Paint the lines on and dust as before.

♣ *Layer 3*: For this layer, you need the smallest cutters. Cut out the tepals, soften the edge and cup them firmly. These tepals are arranged falling further away from the flower centre, but are still cupped, and the lower part of the tepal must still curve to accommodate the stamens and the curves of the previous layers. Paint and dust as before.

Bud: Make a number of pale green claw-shaped buds. These are growth buds. Dust them with a mixture of the greens and catch the top first with a little champagne, and the tiniest touch of the pink mixture at the tip.

♣ Similar-shaped larger buds should also be made.

The buds and growth buds both have a thick neck in pale green. To create this, depending on the size, use $\frac{1}{4}$- or $\frac{1}{2}$-width white tape bound around the wire. Dust with a mix of champagne, apple and vine green.

♣ Tape the layers of tepals together around the central stalk. Using full width white tape, build up a thick section just below the tepals. Dust this as before.

♣ Using the grooved board or rolling pin, roll out the pale green paste and cut the leaves out in various sizes. Insert a moistened 26-gauge green wire. Soften the edges, then vein with the gardenia veiner. Reinforce the central vein by pinching it.

♣ Dust the leaves with green mix and touch the edges with pink mix. Glaze with a $\frac{3}{4}$-glaze.

♣ To wire the branch together, use full width brown tape. On either side of the flowers, tape in two green growth buds. They are arranged alternately, not opposite one another, but very close together. With the addition of each bud, make a heavy ridge on the stem. This is best created by twisting the tape into a thread, building up the ridge and then once again taping over it with the full width tape. The actual flower buds each have their own short branches, often with growth buds. The leaves with their very short stems are usually immediately behind the flowers or buds. Magnolia stems are very ridged.

♣ After taping the flowers, buds and leaves together, dust the stem and add light flecks with an old toothbrush and white paste. Spray with aerosol confectioners' glaze after protecting each flower and bud with kitchen paper.

Curious Cats

15 cm (6 inch) round cake
20 cm (8 inch) cake board
Parchment or greaseproof
paper for making a
template
Airbrush or petal dust and
cotton wool
White royal icing (see
page 139)
No. 0 Bekenal tube
7.5 cm (3 inch) diameter
ball mould

This striking design is just the thing to celebrate the birthday of a cat lover. It looks rather sophisticated as it is but primary colours could be used if it was destined for a child.

✿ Coat the cake with three or more layers of royal icing until you have achieved smooth surfaces on both the top and sides of the cake, with a nice sharp edge. Attach the cake to the board with a little royal icing and ice the board. Set the cake aside until the icing on the board has set.

✿ Cut a piece of cardboard from a thin cake card or cardboard box to fit neatly into a plastic file cover. The type you want is that which has three sides closed; one of the long sides has a reinforced section with holes in it so that they may be filed in a leaver arch file.

✿ Copy the design of the filigree cat from page 142 on to a piece of tracing paper. If you do this and then cut a long tab attached to the tracing, you can start piping over the design at the sealed end of the file cover and gradually move it closer to the open end without damaging any of the previous iced pieces.

✿ Lace pieces can be piped in this same way. This means that you

For a different arrangement, place six more cats joined in a circle on the top of the cake – paws in, tails out – and balance a smaller filigree ball on the upraised paws. If you do not have an airbrush or access to one, use petal dust and cotton wool to complete the stencil design.

need trace only one piece of lace rather than a number of them. The pieces piped this way are more likely to be similar than if you are following lines on many tracings. When piping a filigree piece like this, pipe the outline first, pipe the lines which fill in the design and then neaten the whole thing by piping another outline over all the joins. Keep a just-moist very fine sable brush to hand to neaten any ugly joins.

❧ If you are familiar with this type of work you may decide to pipe only the six cats that are needed to go around the cake. If not, it is advisable to pipe a few more in case of breakages. This would be particularly important if you were using colour in your icing. It is very difficult to mix icing to exactly the same tone if you have run out before the work is complete.

❧ Cut a piece of parchment or greaseproof paper just longer than the circumference of the cake, and the same height as the sides. Trace the cat silhouettes on to this piece of paper, spacing them evenly; remember not to include the join in this measurement. Cut out the silhouettes using a very sharp craft knife and a chopping board for cutting out on. Join the template together to form a collar. Fold it in half and then into three and at the upper edge mark the template lightly. Slide the template over the cake carefully. Make tiny marks on the edge of the cake so you know where the cake is divided into six. Airbrush the colour through the template on to the surface of the cake. If you do not have access to an airbrush, transfer the colour to the side of the cake using cotton

wool and petal dust. Be very careful in both instances not to drop colour on the board.

❧ Remove the template from the side of the cake. Carefully position the shapes cut from the template on the board, between the cats transferred to the side of the cake. A little double-sided sticky tape will hold these pieces in place. Be quite sure you don't have any loose edges that may lift, or the colour will get beneath the masking shapes. Airbrush or dust over the shapes using the same colour as before. Set aside to dry.

❧ Pipe a very fine snailtrail around the base of the cake.

❧ Grease the ball mould and pipe a cornelli design over both halves, keeping the design as loose as possible. Very carefully remove the two shapes from the ball mould. Place one half in a shaped piece of foam rubber that will keep the ball steady while you are joining the two halves together. Once this has dried, pipe very loose loops and swirls over the base to look like a rather untidy ball of wool. Stick this ball into the centre of the cake with small dots of icing near the centre.

❧ Lift a cat off the plastic sleeve, pipe tiny spots of icing on to the paw, the forearm and under the leg and attach to the board at an angle.

❧ You may prefer to place the cake on a larger board and position the cats closer together at right angles to the cake surface. If you choose this method you will need many more of the filigree cats than I have suggested.

❧ Very carefully brush a little of the colour lightly on to the ball surmounting the cake.

5 teaspoons cold water
2 teaspoons powdered
gelatine
500 g (1 lb) icing sugar,
sifted
3 teaspoons gum
tragacanth or
2 teaspoons gum
tragacanth and
2 teaspoons carboxy
methyl cellulose
2 ml teaspoons liquid
glucose
2 teaspoons white fat
white of a size 2 egg

FLOWERPASTE

❦ Measure the cold water into an ovenproof container, sprinkle the gelatine over the surface of the water and leave to stand for 30 minutes.

❦ Sift the icing sugar into the bowl of a heavy-duty mixer. Sprinkle the gum tragacanth (or gum tragacanth and carboxy methyl cellulose) over the surface of the icing. Warm in a pre-heated oven at 100°C/200°F/gas $\frac{1}{4}$ for 30 minutes. The warm sugar keeps the mixture softer and more pliable for longer.

❦ Warm the liquid glucose until it is runny. Dissolve the gelatine and water in the bowl over a pan of hot but not boiling water, or use a microwave. Remove the bowl of gelatine from over the hot water and add the softened glucose and the white fat. Return to a low heat and stir gently until all these ingredients are dissolved and blended together.

❦ Warm the beater of the mixer in hot water, dry and place it in the mixer. Place the bowl of warmed sugar in the mixer. Add the dissolved gelatine mixture and the egg white. Cover the bowl and mixer with a clean, dry cloth and turn the mixer to the slowest speed. Once all the ingredients have been combined, turn the mixer to maximum speed. Beat the paste until it is white and stringy. It is advisable to keep your arm on the upper arm of the mixer to stop the excess movement.

❦ Remove the paste from the bowl and place in a clean plastic bag. Seal and place in an airtight container and refrigerate. The paste is better if it is left to mature for 24 hours before use.

250 g (8 oz/2 cups) icing
sugar, sifted
3 teaspoons gum
tragacanth or 2
teaspoons gum tragacanth
and 2 teaspoons carboxy
methyl cellulose
1 teaspoon liquid glucose
5 teaspoons cold water

MEXICAN PASTE

❦ Sieve the icing sugar and gum tragacanth into a bowl. Warm the jar of liquid glucose in a bowl of hot water; measure the liquid glucose and stir it into a small container containing the cold water. Stir until the liquid glucose dissolves completely in the cold water.

❦ Add the liquid to the dry ingredients, and stir until the two mixtures are combined. Sieve a little icing sugar on to a work surface and knead the paste until it becomes smooth and pliable. If it is too firm, simply add a few drops of cold water, knead again and see if it is as pliable as you would like it. The paste should roll out very easily on a little icing sugar and should have a lovely silky feel to it.

❦ If, however, you are using this recipe for figure modelling, the paste should then be used for this purpose within 24 hours.

❦ The remaining paste may be used for drapes, swags or clothing for animals or figure models. It can be kept for long periods as long as it is kept in a sealed plastic bag, in an airtight container, in the refrigerator.

Note: Any paste being used to create thick items such as rocks, figures, animals or birds, which all take a long time to dry out, may be prone to fermentation. The fermentation can continue for as long as the paste is still partially moist. By that time, surface cracking may have occurred and spoilt the piece. Freshly made paste can reduce this possibility.

*225 g (8 oz) icing sugar,
carefully sifted
1 egg white, size 2
Pinch of tartaric acid or 2
drops acetic acid (the
latter is used for long
dropped lines of extension
work, the former for fine,
firm lace*

This recipe for royal icing is intended only for very fine tubework. For embroidery, brush embroidery, snailtrail, coating, runouts etc. it is preferable to use a dried albumen powder or other dried substitute.

ROYAL ICING

🍀 Sift the icing sugar on to a piece of greaseproof paper.

🍀 Wash the bowl and beater of your food mixer very carefully using a good detergent. Scald the bowl and beater with very hot water to ensure all the detergent is removed. Dry carefully with a clean tea towel.

🍀 Break the egg on to a clean saucer, separating the yolk from the white very carefully. Remove the string from the white. Place the egg white into the bowl, add the tartaric acid or acetic acid, pour about 200 g (7 oz) of the sifted icing sugar into the bowl, and turning the mixer to the slowest possible speed, beat for about 8 minutes.

🍀 Test to see if you have reached full peak (use a clean wooden spoon, dip it into the icing and if it pulls up to a sharp peak it is

ready; if it curves sideways it may need a little more sugar).

🍀 Place in a carefully washed glass bowl, also scalded afterwards and carefully dried. Place cling film directly on to the icing and seal it well against the sides of the bowl. Cover the top of the bowl with another layer of cling film. Cover this with a clean cloth that is only just damp.

🍀 If using a dried albumen or substitute there is no necessity to use an acid to change the pH balance of the egg whites. Oxygenation takes place during the drying process so the alkalinity is altered to suit the making of the royal icing.

🍀 Reconstitute the dried albumen as instructed on the packet, sieve it carefully through a fine sieve to remove undissolved particles then make the icing as instructed above.

There are books on this subject readily available, so having had your interest stirred you might like to study this interesting topic in more depth. It makes old furniture and odd bits and pieces very much more appealing and attractive.

TOLE WORK

🍀 This is a very old form of decoration which has only recently been used on cakes.

🍀 This form of decoration is also known as Folk Art or Bauernmalerei. It is found throughout Europe, decorating farm implements, kitchen cupboards, on old Gipsy caravans and on narrowboats. It is a primitive art form using simple shades and bold but not garish colours.

🍀 A lot of the shapes are symbolic. Circles, sometimes with a dissecting cross or curved lines radiating from the centre, are a sun sign, which is a symbol of life. A series of lines crossing one another vertically and horizontally making a mesh is a symbol of fertility both on land

and in the water. Cross-hatching is a symbol of the womb. Diamond shapes with or without decoration are a symbol of prosperity. The heart is a symbol of love and a leaning to God.

🍀 The flowers most commonly used are the tulip and the rose, often with cross-hatching and dots. Leaves are often curved and rather the same shape as our traditional C scroll.

🍀 I use my usual sable brushes for outlining and painting the scrolls and dots, but I find the most invaluable brush is a 7.5 mm ($\frac{3}{8}$ inch) sable flat brush with fairly long hairs. I load the brush with different colours on either side of the squared end and by curving and twisting it as I paint I get light and shade painted in at the same time.

🍀 I have included a basic plaque

TECHNIQUES

> There is not enough room in this book to more than touch on tole work, but it is something that comes very easily with a little trial and error.

with a design that you might like to try. On the watering can I just 'did my own thing', creating a splash of colour on a dark green background (see Patio Perfection cake on page 62.)

♣ You can use royal icing for this technique – it also works very well in buttercream, but this is best done in bits on a rolled buttercream top or a frozen buttercream base (here you have to keep putting it back in the freezer so the base remains firm!).

♣ You can also buy what has been called 'Folk Art Paint' from a few specialist cake decorating shops. I have used this edible medium on the plaque and also on the watering can.

---

250 g (8 oz/1⅓ cups) glacé cherries (green, red and yellow), halved
1 kg (2 lb) seedless raisins
1 kg (2 lb) stalkless sultanas
250 g (8 oz/1⅓ cups) currants
125 g (4 oz/⅔ cup) glacé pineapple, chopped
125 g (4 oz/1 cup) glacé apricots or dried apricots, chopped
250 g (8 oz/2 cups) split almonds
500 g (1 lb/2 cups) butter
500 g (1 lb/2⅔ cups) dark muscovado sugar
500 g (1 lb/4 cups) plain flour
30 ml (2 tablespoons) apricot jam
30 ml (2 tablespoons) treacle
2.5 ml (½ teaspoon) bicarbonate of soda
2.5 ml (½ teaspoon) ground mace
5 ml (1 teaspoon) each ground ginger, cloves, nutmeg, allspice, cinnamon
10 eggs, size 2
120 ml (4 fl oz/½ cup) brandy
250 g (8 oz/2 cups) ground almonds
500 g (1 lb/2 cups) dates, minced

RICH FRUIT CAKE

This mixture makes 1 × 30 cm (12 inch) square cake, or 1 × 23 cm (9 inch) plus 1 × 18 cm (7 inch) round cakes or 3 × 18 cm (7 inch) round cakes.

♣ Place the cherries, sultanas, raisins and currants into one or two colanders. Rinse under hot running water until the water runs clear. Bang the colander a couple of times and allow to drain for an hour.

♣ Place this fruit plus the chopped pineapple, apricots and split almonds into a large airtight bowl with sealing lid, add the brandy and seal. Shake the bowl vigorously and leave to stand for a week.

♣ Cream the butter and sugar until light and fluffy. Sieve the dry ingredients together. Add the dry ingredients, jam, treacle and eggs alternately, beating well between each addition. Do not add the eggs too quickly or the mixture may curdle. Add the brandy, minced dates and ground almonds, then beat once again. Keep a little of the unfruited batter to one side. Stir the fruit into the remaining batter.

♣ Prepare the cake tin or tins by greasing with butter and lining with silicone or greaseproof paper. Spread a thin layer of unfruited batter in the bottom of the tin, add the fruited batter and finish with a layer of unfruited batter. This allows the fruit to rise into the unfruited batter, and so avoiding bitter, dried fruit standing proud on the top of the cake. Wrap and tie a double layer of brown paper around the outside of the tin.

♣ Bake in a preheated oven at 140°C/275°F/gas 1 for about 6 hours. Test to see if the cake is done after about 5 hours and check regularly until it is ready. The top should spring back if you press on to it and a skewer inserted into the cake should come out clean.

♣ Remove the cake from the oven, cover with a clean tea towel and allow to cool in the tin. Remove from the tin and store carefully wrapped in greaseproof paper and then several layers of foil. This cake is best if allowed to mature for about 3 months before cutting, but is ready to eat immediately if that is necessary.

Note: Always use the best brandy you can afford to buy in your rich fruit cake. Cheating and using a cheap one is a false economy as it could spoil the whole cake!

TEMPLATES

▼ Lace Pieces

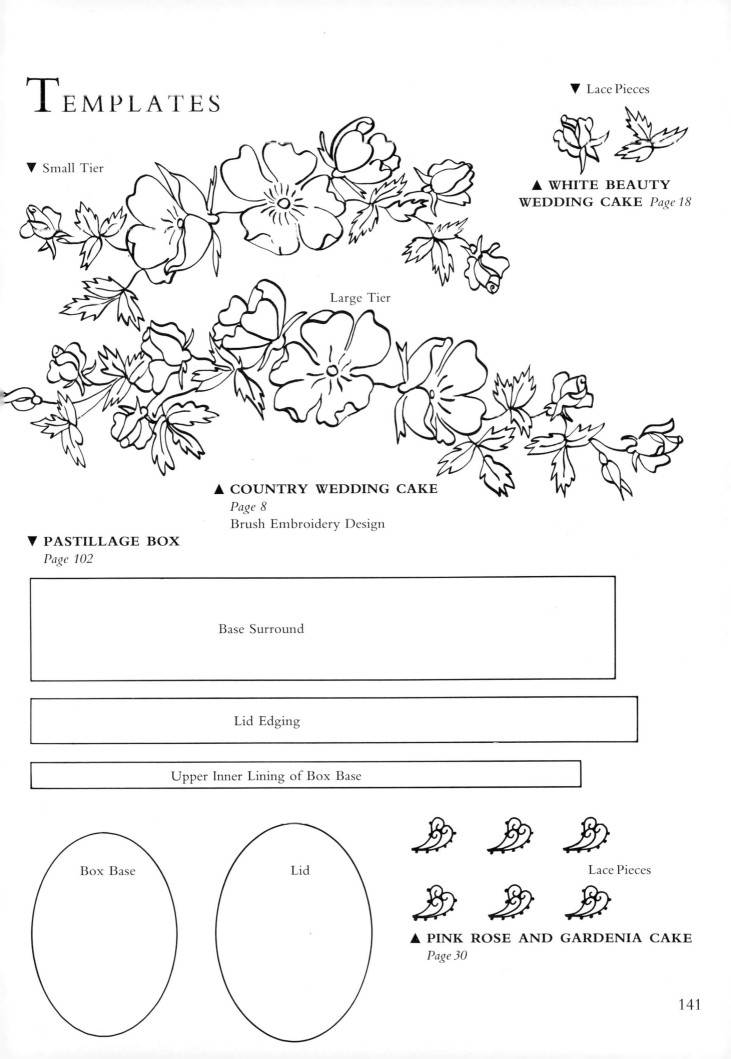

▲ **WHITE BEAUTY
WEDDING CAKE** *Page 18*

▼ Small Tier

Large Tier

▲ **COUNTRY WEDDING CAKE**
Page 8
Brush Embroidery Design

▼ **PASTILLAGE BOX**
Page 102

Base Surround

Lid Edging

Upper Inner Lining of Box Base

Box Base

Lid

Lace Pieces

▲ **PINK ROSE AND GARDENIA CAKE**
Page 30

141

VICTORIAN DECOUPAGE CHRISTENING CAKE
Page 108

Layer 1

Layer 2

Layer 3

Layer 4

Layer 5

▼ **CURIOUS CATS**   *Page 135*

Filigree cat for sides

Silhouette shapes for airbrushing

► **EASTER EGG**
Page 112

◄ **TOLE WORK**
Page 139
A semi traditional
design for a
tole work placemat

Cake line

Line for supporting extension work

DAMASK ROSE CAKE
Page 126

Filet crochet
design

► **MAGNOLIA CAKE**
Page 130

143

INDEX

Acorns, 75, 76
African wedding cake, 48
Agapanthus, 50
All-in-one rose, 44

Beech leaves, 79
Birdsfoot ivy, 17
Bittersweet, 14
Bonsai, 90
   flowering cherry, 91–93
   hazelnut, 97
   wisteria, 94–96
Briar rose, 10
Bridal gladiolus, 56, 57
Brush embroidered magnolia
   cake, 130
Bryony, black, 16
Butterfly, 103

Cake decoration, history of, 4, 5
Chinese jasmine, 35
Chinese lanterns, 68, 69
Christening cake, Victorian
   dècoupage, 108
Christmas rose, 60, 61
Christmas rose cake, 58
Coffee cherry, 39
Coffee flower, 38
Coffee leaves, 39
Country wedding cake, 8
Curious cats, 135
Cyclamen, 118, 119, 120

Damask rose, 128
Damask rose cake, 126
Dark ivy, 16
Dendrobium orchid, 25–27
Devil's root, 53
Dried & pressed flowers, 66, 67
Dried flower arrangement, 68

Easter egg, enamelled, 112
Elephants, moulded, 109, 110
Enamelled Easter egg, 112
Engagement cake, hearts and
   flowers, 109
Erica, 54, 55
Eucalyptus leaves, 52

Filet crochet extension work,
   127
Flowering cherry
   bonsai, 91–93
   bud, 93
   leaves, 93
Flowerpaste, 138
   Victorian dècoupage, 106
Fly honeysuckle, 13

Forget-me-nots, 83
Freesia, 42
Fuchsia, 83

Gardenia
   bud, 34
   leaves, 34
   wired, 32–34
Garrett frill/flounce, 117
Gladiolus, bridal, 56, 57

Harvest cake, 72
Hazel leaves, 98
Hazelnuts 98
   bonsai, 97
Hearts and flowers engagement
   cake, 109
Honesty, 77
   flower, 78
   leaves, 78
   unpeeled seedheads, 78
Honeysuckle, 12, 13

Ivy
   birdsfoot, 17
   dark, 16
   variegated, 16

Japanese honeysuckle, 13
Jasmine
   Chinese, 35
   Madagascan, 20, 21
Java orchid, 47

Larch cones, 74
Lily
   bud, 55
   longiflorum, 28
Lily-of-the-valley, quick, 46
Longiflorum lily, 28
Lotus seedheads, 70

Madagascan jasmine, 20, 21
Magnolia, 132
   buds, 134
   leaves, 134
Magnolia cake, 130
Mexican paste, 138
Mother's Day gift, 116, 117

Nasturtium, 64

Oak leaves, 79
Orchid
   dendrobium, 25–27
   Java, 47

Painted lady, 56, 57
Pansy, 82, 83
Passion flower, 104
Passion flower cake, 103
Pastillage

making, 102
   oval box, 102
   passion flower cake, 103
   pressed flower card, 84
   trinket bowl, 85, 86
   Victorian découpage, 106
Patio perfection, 62
Pearl grass, 70
Periwinkle, 9
Physalis, 68, 69
Pink rose and gardenia wedding
   cake, 30
Pleated drape, 126
Poppy seedheads, 71
Porcelaine wedding cake, 40
Potentilla, 83
Pressed flower card, 84
Pressed flowers, 80, 82
Primrose, 83

Quaking grass, 70

Rich fruit cake, 140
Rose, 21–24
   all-in-one, 44
   Christmas, 60, 61
   damask, 128
   porcelaine, 40
Rose hips, 709
Rosy cheeked lovebirds, 51
Royal icing, 139
Ruscus, 27

Shepherd's delight, 56
Silver tree, 52
Stephanotis, 20, 21
Sugarpaste
   Mother's Day gift, 116, 117
   waterlily pram cake, 121

Templates, 141–143
Tole work, 139
Trinket bowl, 85, 86
Twigs, 72

Variegated ivy, 16
Victorian découpage
   Christening cake, 108
   flowerpaste, 106
   pastillage, 106
Viola, 82, 83

Waterfall sprays, wiring, 36
Waterlily pram cake, 121
Wedding cakes
   African, 48
   country, 8
   pink rose and gardenia, 30
   porcelaine, 40
   white beauty, 18
White beauty wedding cake, 18
Wisteria bonsai, 94–96